I-2-I
DISCIPLESHIP

Christine Dillon

ISBN 978-1-84550-425-0

Copyright © Christine Dillon 2009

10 9 8 7 6 5 4 3 2 1

Published in 2009,
Reprinted in 2010
by
OMF Publishing
Station Approach, Borough Green,
Sevenoaks, Kent, TN15 8BG
www.omf.org.uk
and
Christian Focus Publications, Ltd.,
Geanies House, Fearn, Ross-shire,
IV20 1TW, Great Britain.

www.christianfocus.com

Copyright material is used by permission of OMF International

Cover design by Daniel Van Straaten
Printed by Bell and Bain, Glasgow

Mixed Sources
Product group from well-managed
forests and other controlled sources
www.fsc.org Cert no.TT-COC-002769
© 1996 Forest Stewardship Council

Contents

DEDICATION

Thank you to Jeff, Beth and Andy from whom I am learning what it means to follow Christ.

Thank you to the many people who I've had the privilege of discipling and for your patience with the many mistakes I probably made along the way. This book is possible because of what you've taught me and I rejoice to see each of you growing more like Jesus.

Thank you Mum and Dad for taking time to disciple your own children even though we were often far apart.

Thank you to my colleagues in OMF who have supported me in discipling others and allowed me time to write; to Phil, David, Richard and Andy; to Rebecca who has been a constant encouragement to a fledgling author.

Last but definitely not least I wish to thank Jesus. Following Him has been an adventure and a delight. He is the one who has taught me everything I've learnt so far. I look forward to learning more.

PREFACE

It has often been said, 'the Church in Africa is a mile wide and an inch deep.' But why has Africa been singled out? A similar comment could be made about much of Asia, Europe or the West. Or perhaps even a less complimentary observation more along the lines of 'a tenth of a mile wide and still only an inch deep.'

Lack of depth and maturity in the worldwide church is a major problem. Very few Christians really know their Bibles well or can apply the Word to their daily lives. Few really live as 'salt and light' in a dark world. Most make little impact for the Kingdom or know how to share their faith simply and in such a way that people want to listen. Sadly many are not even aware their Christian lives could be any different and so they live frustrated lives.

Where has the church gone wrong?

Could it be that we have failed to follow what Jesus commanded? His very last command before He returned to heaven was very simple 'Go and make disciples of all nations, baptising them in the name of the Father, Son and Spirit and teaching them all I have commanded you. And surely I am with you even to the end of the age' (Matt. 28:19-20).

A person's last words before they die or leave should be important and Jesus certainly wasn't going to waste the opportunity when His disciples were listening so intently. Of all the things that Jesus could have said, He commanded, 'go and make disciples'. There is no mention of making church buildings or setting up denominations or ordaining church leaders or attending Bible college or even of getting lots of people 'to make decisions' for Christ.

Make disciples – Jesus knew that if His disciples did that, then all else that might be necessary (such as having church leaders) would follow on. If we get the discipling part right then the church will grow and the church can become wide AND deep, giving life and refreshment instead of only disappointment and frustration.

This book aims to explain what discipleship is and give practical guidelines for discipling others. I feel compelled to write it because few seem to have been discipled themselves and good books on the topic seem surprisingly scarce. I was one of those who had to learn everything by trial and error. This book is the kind that I was looking for but didn't find. I hope this might ensure your way is a little easier.

This book doesn't claim to be entirely comprehensive or to have the last word on how things should be done. No doubt in the future, with more experience and further insight, I will disagree with some of what I have written here. But hopefully it will pass on some of the things I have learnt and help you to at least get started in discipling.

And this booklet is supposed to be practical! So make sure you do the activities as you go through. It is always tempting to skip the tasks but they are the sections that will most help you apply what you've learnt and prepare you to disciple someone else. Please also pray as you go, that God will use you for His glory to disciple others.

Christine Dillon

PART ONE:

UNDERSTANDING DISCIPLESHIP

1 : What Is a Disciple?

Thousands of years ago it was common to see a wandering teacher or philosopher surrounded by his disciples: Confucius in China or Aristotle in Greece. A disciple was one who wanted to learn and be influenced by a certain teacher. They often lived alongside that teacher and spent their days listening and discussing issues.

Jesus' disciples were the same. Twelve were especially known as 'the Disciples' but in fact there were others who were also discipled including women like Mary Magdalene, Susanna and Joanna (Luke 8:2-3). They followed Jesus as He travelled around Israel, listening to His teaching and observing His lifestyle.

A secular dictionary defines 'disciple' as 'somebody who strongly believes in the teachings of a leader, a philosophy, or a religion, and tries to act according to them'[1]. Christians have a huge advantage over other kinds of disciples. The source of our strength is God Himself and so we don't just 'try' to imitate Jesus, we can increasingly succeed.

Lynn Anderson's definition is succinct: a disciple is a 'following learner'[2]. This definition implies not only spending significant time with the one we want to be like, but also actively

---

1   *Encarta World English Dictionary.* 1999. Microsoft Corporation (Developed for Microsoft by Bloomsbury Publishing).

2   Lynn Anderson, quoted in *The Case for Faith*, Lee Strobel. Zondervan, 2000.

choosing to learn. Jesus defined a disciple by saying, 'If you hold to my teaching you are really my disciples' (John 8:31b).

John Stott defines a disciple as 'someone who is on the lifetime process of having their character transformed and moulded to Jesus' will'[3]. His definition focuses on Christian character, becoming more and more like Jesus. That is, increasingly patient, loving, gentle, trustworthy and joyful. Disciples want to become like Jesus in purpose, attitudes and values. 2 Corinthians 3:18 refers to the disciples as 'we who with unveiled faces all reflect the Lord's glory, [and] are being transformed into his likeness with ever-increasing glory.' It is in following Jesus that He unleashes the potential of who we were created to be. It should not be small changes but a radical transformation of our entire lives.

Gary Kuhne includes both a character element and a skills component in his definition, 'a Christian who is growing in conformity to Christ, is achieving fruit in evangelism and is working in follow-up to conserve his fruit'[4]. Jesus Himself said, 'I am the vine and you are the branches. If a man remains in me and I in him, he will bear much fruit; apart from me he can do nothing…. this is to my Father's glory that you bear much fruit, showing yourselves to be my disciples' (John 15:5, 8).

Some people seem to imply that there are different levels of commitment, as though we can choose to be an A, B, or C standard. Jesus' view was radical. You are either a disciple (any Christian) or you are not (a non-Christian). He warns us up front: 'If *anyone* would come after me, he must deny himself, take up his cross and follow me' (Mark 8:34b). To be a disciple of Jesus means a 100% commitment. If we are not willing to die to our own ambitions and dreams and live fully for Christ then we are not Jesus' disciples.

Thus, being a disciple includes developing in knowledge, character, attitudes and skills. The aim of discipleship is Christian maturity.

3   J. R. W. Stott. *Basic Christianity*. Inter-Varsity Press, 1971.

4   G.W. Kuhne. *The Dynamics of Personal Follow-Up*. Zondervan, 1976.

In this book, we will use the following definitions:

> *A Disciple*: A follower of Jesus who is becoming increasingly like Him.
> *Discipleship*: The process of becoming more like Jesus, as we are transformed by the Holy Spirit.

But, if all Christians are Jesus' disciples, what does it mean for us to 'disciple' another Christian?

All Christians are Jesus' disciples and are in the process of discipleship with Him, being changed and renewed by the Holy Spirit. But we, as Jesus' disciples, have a role to play in helping those around us as they are in this discipleship process.

Elisha and Timothy were both followers of God, but they were learning how to be so by observing Elijah and Paul, and how they followed God. Paul urged, 'Imitate me as I am imitating Christ' (1 Cor. 11:1 NASB). His words may seem arrogant but they show how seriously Paul took his responsibility to disciple others and to be worth imitating.

So, we can add the following definition:

> *Discipling*: the meeting of one Christian with one or more others, for the purpose of encouraging them in their spiritual growth to be more like Jesus.

2: Types of Discipling

Helping people grow in Christ can be done in many different ways. Obviously part of the purpose of church services is to help Christians mature. Some Christians will grow in any situation because of the kind of people they are and their learning style. Others may sit in church for twenty years and learn practically nothing; they may find it hard to learn just by being spoken at, they may have educational difficulties, or maybe the preacher simply doesn't communicate well. As well as in the main services, discipling could happen in Bible study groups, Sunday School, women's/men's meetings, camps or on a one-to-one basis.

Group discipling has several advantages:

1. People tend to feel more at home in a group and able to participate without feeling put on the spot.
2. Groups can be fluid, with individuals able to move in and out, so a more relaxed commitment is possible.
3. Bible study can be more dynamic in a group as many share their understandings and applications, and momentum and enthusiasm can grow as members of the group encourage one another.
4. General correction and exhortation can be more easily and subtly done than in a one-to-one context.

But while group discipling can be very beneficial and an effective way to encourage several Christians towards maturity together, one-to-one discipleship is unparalleled in the impact it can make on a Christian's growth.

One-to-one discipleship is advantageous in many ways:

1. Tailor-made

One-to-one ministry can be adapted to fit the individual's needs exactly. Even studying the same passage, different individuals will raise different questions, will wish to cover the text at different speeds and will be challenged in different areas. Even brand-new Christians will be at very different stages. Some may have done five years of Bible study before they became Christians and know the Bible better than you do, while others may have made a decision to follow Jesus on the basis of very little knowledge. One-to-one discipleship gives the opportunity to answer questions, make direct application and deal with personal issues. The one-to-one approach can make a person feel like the Bible was written for them, and can take into account existing knowledge, learning style, personal situation, even the number of questions a disciple likes to ask!

2. Flexible

A group meeting necessitates a set time, place and structure. One-to-one, by contrast, can be very flexible, making it more suitable for those with busy families, shift work or other less predictable arrangements. We can shorten or lengthen the study to accommodate the amount of time the disciple has free.

As I am a person who likes schedules I generally try to have a set time with those I'm discipling as this helps me to organize my week. However, I try not to fill up my time completely, so that I have plenty of space available should a disciple need to change the time we meet. I don't want to be so busy that the disciple feels they can never find me. The flexibility of one-to-one discipleship also allows us to deal with crises or opportunities as they come up.

3. Communicates love and care

So many of those I've discipled have been nearly overwhelmed that I would consider them precious enough to spend individual time with them. So many people are used to a world where even their parents never had time for them. They are in big classes at school and even bigger ones at university. Many are reduced to pouring out their pain and energy to complete strangers on the internet. One-to-one discipleship tells them they are precious to both us and God.

4. In-depth

In a one-to-one setting we are able to be more 'in-depth' in our discussion, not worrying if the topic is missing some and confusing others. We are also able to cover far more in a much shorter time. We can be completely focused on the individual's needs and questions. Being more in-depth and personal might threaten some people, but altering the format of our discipleship and being sensitive in our questioning style should overcome the problem.

5. Closeness

Discipling requires openness and accountability. These are more likely to develop in a situation of closeness and trust, and these in turn are more easily established in a one-to-one setting. One-to-one also makes it easier to avoid a 'teacher-student' relationship. It is very important that from the start we are communicating that discipling is a mutual encouragement situation. This understanding can be emphasised by continual sharing of what we are learning, so it is not just a teacher imparting knowledge and skills to a pupil.

6. Less embarrassment

Many feel embarrassed in a group setting and may be unwilling to ask questions or admit failings in case they appear 'stupid' in front of others. A one-to-one setting can alleviate this anxiety, especially if the discipler is open about their own struggles.

Issues will come to the surface more readily in a one-to-one context, and will also be more easily addressed and dealt with in the privacy of this setting.

7. Life impact

One-to-one discipling is a successful way to model the Christian life in action. As two spend time together, they will quickly learn each other's habits and attitudes, both positive and negative. For example, if the discipler always turns off their mobile phone when they're doing one-to-one, then the disciple should also experience and learn to appreciate the importance of spending uninterrupted time with people. The one-to-one setting can also give the disciple the opportunity to learn skills such as how to confront others, how to understand the Bible for themselves, how to encourage others and how to pray.

8. Reproducible

One-to-one discipleship is easier for people to get involved in. Because it is flexible, nearly everyone has the time to get involved. And because it is more low-key and doesn't require standing up in front of people or having others watch you, it is often a less stressful way of getting involved in ministry. In addition, it doesn't require years of training to meet up with someone and ask how they are getting on. Simply going for a walk or out for coffee with another believer could be a form of discipling! And once someone has been discipled it is relatively easy for them to start discipling someone else.

Many churches have group discipleship programmes, but one-to-one discipleship is largely neglected. Because of this, and the impact one-to-one discipleship could make on Christian growth, although both group and individual discipleship have their place in the Christian life, this book will primarily deal with discipleship on a one-to-one basis.

Reflection:

1. Looking over the chapter, which reasons for group or individual discipleship affect you most strongly? Why? Any you'd like to add?

3: Types of One-to-One Discipling

Good biblical examples of one-to-one discipleship are the relationships between Elijah and Elisha and Paul and Timothy. The younger men travelled with the older, having many opportunities to hear their teaching and to watch them minister to others. They may have had designated sessions for study together, but Elisha and Timothy also lived and worked alongside their teachers in order to learn from them. They would have observed the elder men's prayer habits and seen how they handled opposition and suffering. They would also have been influenced by their teacher's values and ways of talking and thinking, and would have had opportunities to practise the skills they needed to eventually take over from their teachers.

As these relationships show, there are different ways we can disciple someone one-to-one. The possibilities are endless! We'll divide the options into two main categories:

1. Formal Discipling

Formal discipling has the specific aim of coming together to study the Bible and help each other grow in maturity. The meetings are intentional, ongoing and planned in order to achieve specific aims. For example we may organise to meet a new believer to cover the basics of Christianity, or we may plan a six-week course of sessions in order to study a book of the Bible with another member of our church. These formal sessions could include going to workshops or conferences together, but there will be some overarching aim in attending these together, and we will have intentionally planned to attend in order to achieve this purpose.

2. Informal Discipling

This could be anything we do that encourages another person in their relationship with God. It needn't be planned beforehand and could be a one-off opportunity such as having a passing conversation at a bus stop or recommending a book to a stranger in the bookshop.

I met a Mainland Chinese Christian in Sydney airport when our plane was delayed. He said he had been a Christian for a while but had never understood how the Bible fitted together. We took the opportunity to run through a Bible overview briefly before our plane arrived. I never heard from him again but I am sure the two hours we spent impacted his Christian life.

On camps and conferences, for example, we may spend a week sharing with and teaching others. We may have conversations while doing other activities, be involved in a practical ministry together, or simply be living alongside them. The camp ends and we both go home. There is no continued meeting or discussion, but the time we had together helped them grow in maturity. I work in Taiwan and each year groups of young people come over on short-term mission trips. We will spend up to a month living and working together, studying the Bible together and practising ministry skills. Many of these times are life-changing.

We may have informal opportunities with someone we are also meeting on a formal basis. For example, a disciple may ask to meet up because a crisis has arisen, like the death of a friend or a relationship break-up. They may ring to ask how to respond to a question a non-Christian friend has asked about the Bible.

These sessions are not planned or structured, but because of our involvement the person grows in their faith. Flexibility and sensitivity to grasp such are essential opportunities.

Simply going out for coffee and chatting about Jesus and your Christian life, going to the park and discussing issues as you walk, serving in the community together, having a discussion as you drive somewhere or chatting about an experience the disciple has had and reflecting on what happened and how God could be working, are all ways of discipling others. I try to think of every telephone call and letter as a discipleship opportunity and not as an interruption. This doesn't mean I always talk about Jesus but that the way I answer and the time I spend should at the very least communicate God's values. For example, 'you are important and precious'.

So there are many ways that one-to-one discipling can be done, and the most effective will probably be a combination of formal and informal meetings. We will need to rely on the Holy Spirit to help us see what is best. But it is formal discipling, and the many ways we can get involved in it, that we will mainly be looking at in this book.

===

Reflection:
1. What would you add to either the 'formal' or 'informal' category?
2. Write your own summary of each.
3. Think about someone you minister to – identify the various kinds of discipleship you're doing with them. What improvements could be made?

4:
WHAT IS THE GOAL OF DISCIPLING?

J. B Phillips in his New Testament paraphrase[1] describes the aim of discipleship:

> 'So naturally we proclaim Christ! We warn everyone we meet, and we teach everyone we can all that we know about him, so that, if possible, we may bring people up to their full maturity in Jesus Christ. This is what I am working at all the time, with all the strength that God gives me' (Col. 1:28-29).

Let's look at some other biblical images of what we are trying to achieve in discipleship.

Have a look at these verses:

1: A Growing Baby
1 Corinthians 3: 1-2, Hebrews 5: 12-14, 1 Peter 2:2
- What do we expect of a baby?
- How long should someone remain a baby?

The role of the discipler is to 'feed' the young believers from God's Word, helping the disciples to apply it to their lives. The goal is for the new Christian to mature into an adult who is able to be independent and teach others.

---

1   J. B. Phillips. *The New Testament in Modern English*. Collins, 1958.

2: A Fruit-Bearing Tree
Matthew 7:16-20, Luke 8:5-15, John 15:1-8,
Galatians 5:22-23
- What are our 'roots' as Christians?
- What is the ultimate aim for a tree?

The discipler's role is to make sure the plant is watered and well-rooted. Eventually the tree will produce fruit and by this fruit we will know whether the tree is good or bad.

3: Being Refined Like Gold
Psalm 66:10, Daniel 12:10, Zechariah 13:9, Malachi 3:2-3,
1 Peter 1:6-7
- How is our faith purified?
- Will growth be easy?

God uses suffering and discipline in our lives to refine and purify us and produce genuine and firm faith. The discipler's role is to challenge the disciple and help them apply God's truth to their lives, supporting them through situations that may be painful, in order that they may grow as a Christian.

The next two images are not direct Biblical images, but I have found them helpful:

4: Being a Link in the Chain
1 Corinthians 3:5-8, Daniel 1-4
- What part can discipling play in a Christian's growth?
- What is our role and impact as a discipler?

The whole length of chain represents someone's life. The cross represents the time when someone became a Christian. For some, that point is very clear and they can give a date and time. For others it is less defined, although at some point they can look back and know that they are now a 'new creature in Christ' even if they weren't sure exactly when the new birth happened.

The black links to the left of the cross represent the part of our lives when we were non-Christians, when we were 'walking in darkness' (Isa. 9:2, 50:10; John 1:5, 8:12; Eph. 5:8) or 'death' (Eph. 2:1). The white links on the right side of the cross represent our 'new life' and our growth in maturity as a disciple of Jesus. Each link is something or someone that God uses to bring us closer to Himself. A link could be a person, a period of suffering or a book we have read. Not all of these will have had the same amount of impact, so the links could be different sizes, but all have brought us on in spiritual maturity. I leave the links the same size because humans are not very good at judging the relative importance of all these links!

Often Christians focus on getting people to 'make decisions' and cross the line between death and life, thinking this is the beginning and the end of our role. Many brand-new Christians are left to look after themselves. We are excited by the new Christian but we fail to follow up with the same vigour. This could be the reason why so many new Christians never make it to maturity. It is in a baby's nature to grow, and if it does not, it means something is drastically wrong. Immature Christians weigh down the church, prevent the church from working and stop more new Christians being born. The chain diagram reminds us that evangelism and discipleship are part of the same process, and not just a one-off event. How long that process takes depends on God. We will probably never know how many links will take someone to maturity because even in our own lives our view is so limited, but we are responsible for caring for and nurturing younger Christians.

5: Replacing Untruth with Truth
2 Corinthians 10:5, Acts 10

- Is it only non-Christians that hold untrue beliefs?
- How are our beliefs changed?

Each brick represents an idea or belief that we hold on to that is not true. Although different people may have similar bricks in their lives, especially within one culture or religious background, everyone's bricks will be slightly different.

These bricks prevent us from hearing and believing the truth shown in God's Word. The wall stops the person from hearing the gospel. Have you ever had the experience of sharing the gospel with someone and it is like 'talking to a brick wall'?

During a lifetime, God uses many things to challenge our thinking. My goal in sharing with anyone, Christian or not, is always to try to work out what bricks are in someone's life and then share the truth in a way that allows God's Word to challenge those bricks.

It is important to remember that discipleship is not just about our words but our actions, and the way we treat people and react to situations. If one of the bricks in a person's life is 'Christians are boring' then their thinking will be challenged by seeing Christians who enjoy life and have it abundantly.

Breaking down the brick wall begins before the person is a Christian. Changing the bricks from lies to truth is a lifetime process. We will never have a perfect 'wall of truth' until heaven. Humans are very blind and, although we become Christians, God still has many things He'll need to change before we think like He does.

A friend of mine, Irene, had been a Christian for four years. She lived in the southern part of Taiwan and had come out of a Buddhist/Taoist, idol-worshipping background. One of the beliefs that she firmly held was that it is the responsibility of the gods to make life pleasant and smooth. When she became a Christian she carried this thinking over into her new life. She was surprised and upset when being a Christian proved so much hard work. In fact, there seemed to be more suffering since she became a Christian than before. Now, on top of all the normal stresses of life, she found that her family opposed her new decision and pressured her to continue ancestor worship. Her workmates also started to ridicule her new faith. She could no longer tell lies to protect herself and so got in trouble more often. These problems caused lots of doubts. After 18 months of discipleship and continual discussion of such books as 1 Peter and Habakkuk, Irene began to glimpse the truth that suffering is normal for anyone living on this earth; also that suffering is even more the lot of Christians, whom Satan and his followers hate. Through the stories of Joseph, Jesus and Paul she came to see that God works out His purposes through suffering. Slowly she began to say with Habakkuk: 'though the figtree does not blossom …' (3:17) though nothing goes right ... 'I will still choose to trust in God and rejoice'. For the rest of her life she will struggle with this issue. As she increasingly matures it will be evident by how she faces suffering. Will she complain or accept it as a gracious gift from a loving Heavenly Father? Will she rejoice?

For a new Christian there will be many areas linked with our views and values that God needs to change, issues linked with money, relationships, work, ministry, time and priorities. We will need to learn so much about people, sin, the future (heaven, hell and judgment) and what it means to be a Christian. There is a lifetime of maturing that needs to take place. God can do much of this transforming as we are discipled and then as we disciple others.

Remember, though, a person does not mature because of our work. Yes, God might choose to work through us but He is the one who transforms lives (1 Cor. 3:6). We must also remember that it will take a lot of time and energy to grow from immature to mature in Christ. A fruit tree takes years to grow to maturity. A human baby takes decades to become an adult and then keeps maturing all its life. We will not reach full maturity as Christians until we get to heaven.

DISCIPLESHIP MUST SHAPE CHARACTER

Our actions result from the overflow of our hearts (Mark 7:20-23). If our attitudes and motivations are godly, then our words and deeds will flow out from there and be godly too. Throughout the Bible God constantly rejected hypocritical behaviour where the outside seemed very religious but the heart was far away from God. Jesus went so far as to say to the Pharisees, 'You are like whitewashed tombs, which look beautiful on the outside but on the inside are full of dead men's bones and everything unclean' (Matt. 23:27). Those religious leaders had fooled everyone else but they couldn't fool God.

If our deeds and our character don't match, eventually people will dismiss our deeds. When discipling others, we need to remember that transferring skills is of secondary importance to growing increasingly like Jesus.

How then can we encourage real heart changes and not merely outward changes? Growing increasingly like Jesus is the purpose of discipleship, so how can we encourage people to be like Jesus to the very core of their being?

Here are some hints:

1. Feed the 'Roots'

The 'fruit' will develop naturally as the roots are nurtured. As they get to know Jesus better and become more and more excited about who Jesus is and what He has done for them, they will 'reflect his likeness with ever-increasing glory' (2 Cor. 3:18).

Building good foundations will result in a stronger building in the end.

2. Use the Sword

We need to teach disciples to use the 'Sword of the Spirit, which is the Word of God' (Eph. 6:17). Every thought that comes into their head must be compared with God's truth. If it is not a godly thought then they must remind themselves about what God says on the matter.

3. Replace, don't just Remove

Ephesians 4:22-28 describes us as needing to 'take off' the old, dirty clothes (habits, attitudes and behaviours) and 'put on' new ones. For example, we're told to 'take off' anger and 'put on' forgiveness (v. 26), to 'take off' stealing and 'put on' generosity instead (v. 28). Don't just look at what we shouldn't be doing, but discuss how to achieve what we should be doing.

4. Prepare for Suffering

Many people nowadays want God to be like a divine Santa Claus, making life easy for us. They want an indulgent parent instead of a loving and responsible one. But we need to remember that God is primarily concerned about our maturity as Christians and not about making our lives easy. Mark 8:34 tells us that if we want to be disciples, we must 'take up our cross and follow him.' This means dying to our own values and ambitions which will inevitably be hard work. We must prepare disciples to persevere through tough and painful experiences that will ultimately help us grow in faith. Even when we are being fruitful in our Christian lives, God promises, 'every branch that does bear fruit he prunes so that it will be even more fruitful' (John 15:2). God prunes us by rebuking, correcting and training us through His Word and by continually pointing out areas of our characters we need to work on, and putting us in situations where we are forced to address these issues. God has promised we will go through the fire in order to be refined like gold, and

31

we need to prepare disciples to expect this and to be able to work through the difficulties to achieve real character change.

5. Achieve Balance

Although it is most important that our characters are transformed, and right actions will flow when we become increasingly like Jesus, we need to have the opportunity to put what we have learnt into practice. Spending all our time taking in and never giving out is likely to cause us to stagnate as Christians. To achieve real heart changes, we need to be putting into practice what God is teaching us. We need to help disciples to see the outworkings of being a disciple. Be warned though, if we are to bear fruit for God, there must be a balance between our spending time with God and our service of others. Because God is unseen, He is far easier to ignore than the numerous situations in front of us demanding our attention. As a result we will often end up serving more than we end up spending time alone with God. In the long term, this will result in spiritual dryness, as we neglect to drink the 'living water'. Balance in Christian ministry means we have time for rest and relaxation. It quickly becomes obvious when we are not balanced in these areas.

Reflection:

1. Do a 'links in the chain' diagram for your life.
2. What 'bricks' in your life did God have to change before you became a Christian?
3. Can you see any areas that still need work as you are discipled?
4. What has been your attitude to suffering up to this point? Reflect on this sentence: 'It's not what happens to us, but our response to what happens to us that either builds or harms our character.'
5. What areas of balance do you struggle with most? Why? What do you need to do to correct the balance?

5: GOD'S DISCIPLESHIP

—

OUR DISCIPLING

Peggy admitted that one of the reasons that she was always late for church was because she was terrified of the pastor's wife. The pastor's wife would often chastise, 'If you really loved God you'd be here early,' or 'You really should be baptized by now'.

The youth group were also unenthusiastic and it turned out that nearly all those who had been baptized had done so out of fear of the pastor's wife. Very few were clear what baptism meant and many weren't even believers.

The pastor's wife was trying to grow fruit by nagging and pressurising. She wanted to see young people following Jesus and being committed to the church but she was going about it in completely the wrong way. She had confused her role and God's.

GOD'S ROLE

Only God can raise the spiritually dead. No matter what we do or say, we can never, in our own power, make someone become a Christian. In the same way, only God can bring growth in a disciple's life. We might be involved in watering, preparing the soil, or fertilizing but we haven't any power to make the plants grow (1 Cor. 3:5-8).

Why is it so important to get this clear?

If we begin to think that we are able to raise the spiritually dead or make Christians mature in our own strength then we will never achieve any lasting results. And in the process we will exhaust ourselves trying to come up with new methods to produce better results, and spend lots of energy and money trying to find the key to making people come to Christ and grow. There are ways we can learn to communicate better, but it is the communication of God's Word and the work of the Spirit that bring about results.

People who have confused their role with God's believe that the results of ministry are somehow related to them. They may be excessively interested in how to measure spiritual growth, counting how many went through the baptism classes, discipleship programmes and evangelism training. Many of these activities are useful but we need to be careful that we don't encourage people to be involved for our own reasons. If our motivation is to feed our ego or convince others that we're doing our job properly, then we're on the top of a 'slippery slope' that will only lead to disaster. Frustration will build because we can't get people to do what we want.

Also, be warned, some people will grow whatever programme they go through, because of God's grace and their ability to learn even if it was a wholly negative learning situation, and this may convince us that we're doing the right thing. It isn't hard for us to fool ourselves and dismiss all the people who don't grow or eventually leave the church as 'drop outs' and 'not grateful for all that's done for them'.

If a tree is good then the fruit grows naturally! The key to getting people to be baptized, enthusiastic and committed to church is not pressure and manipulation but encouragement to know and love Jesus more. If there is no new life in a person, they will never produce real fruit. They might mimic the fruit by being baptized and coming to church, but they are still spiritually dead. As a Christian grows, the root is strengthened, and they want to be baptized and to spend more time with other Christians.

So if God is the one who raises the spiritually dead and brings about growth, what is our role?

It would seem we are not needed at all! After all, if God is able to do everything and does it perfectly, why bother with us? That is one of the mysteries and wonders of God's methods. For some reason, we cannot do the work of discipleship independently from God, but He has chosen to do His work through weak human beings. In fact, the weaker the better from His point of view, because then 'no-one may boast before Him' (1 Cor. 1:27-29). The weaker we are the more obvious it is that all our achievements are God's.

Our Role

1. To Pray

This is something God can't do for us. He can give us the motivation and strength to pray, He can even tell us what to pray for, but in the end only we can do the hard work of prayer.

We catch glimpses of the importance of prayer in discipleship in Paul's letters, where he uses phrases such as 'I pray that you may ...' and 'My heart's desire and prayer is ...' Although Paul was usually far away from the churches he wrote to, he never forgot them and continued to pray fervently for them.

What Paul prayed for gives us guidance as to what to pray for those we disciple:

- He remembered to **thank God** constantly for the Christians (Rom. 1:8, 1 Cor. 1:4f, Phil. 1:3f, Col. 1:3f, 1 Thess. 1:2f and many more).
- He **prayed for their spiritual growth**, not only in knowledge, but in understanding and application (Eph. 1:15ff, 3:16ff, 2 Tim. 1).
- He **prayed for their witness** to a non-Christian world (Philem. 6).

Prayer is the one thing we'll easily forget or be tempted to cut out of our schedule. To do so is to impoverish our lives and ministry.

2. To Teach

As Timothy began to take on his own disciples, Paul urged him, 'All Scripture is God-breathed and is useful for teaching, rebuking, correcting and training in righteousness … be prepared in season and out of season: correct, rebuke and encourage with great patience and careful instruction' (2 Tim. 3:16, 4:2). We have the same responsibility as Timothy in discipleship, and it is not a small one!

Because the Bible is the Word of God, we can never be casual about our teaching of it. The nature of discipleship means that we will have a big influence in another Christian's life, and we must be careful not to abuse it by the way we teach the Bible. Careless, skewed or wrong teaching may have a devastating impact.

Paul also reminds us that discipleship is not just about teaching the meaning of God's Word, but about rebuking, counselling, encouraging and training, which will take great patience and care. God's role in all this will be in giving us wisdom and discernment and making us increasingly godly, so we can be patient, loving and committed to prayer.

3. To Remain Dependent

Discipleship, like any ministry, is one that comes from the overflow of our own relationship with God and unless we remain dependent on God, failure is inevitable. Our dependence shows itself in constant prayer and feeding on God's Word. We are the car and God is the fuel. We might be able to keep going for a very short time without the fuel but we are deceiving ourselves if we think it is truly possible to be independent of God.

The Sea of Galilee and the Dead Sea in Israel are related to the Jordan River system. However, if you were to visit them you would see no similarity. One is beautiful and full of life and the other is full of salt, minerals and death. What's the difference? A river flows into and out of the Sea of Galilee, but only flows into and then stagnates in the Dead Sea. Like these two seas, for life and growth, we need both inflow and outflow. If we only take in teaching but don't serve, like the Dead Sea, we will start to stagnate and die. Equally, if the water only flows out, a sea soon ceases to exist. If we are to disciple effectively we must be taking in as we give out.

4. To Be Worth Following

'Caught rather than taught' is a useful way of describing the process of discipleship. A disciple will become like their discipler in many ways. We must make sure that we are worth following and that we can say, with Paul, 'imitate me as I imitate Christ' (1 Cor. 11:1 NASB). Paul was able to say it because he knew he was following Jesus so closely. Disciples will learn how to deal with conflict, encourage others, evangelise and so on because of how they see us doing these things, more than because of what they heard us say about these topics.

5. To Minister Sacrificially

Jesus spent three years and nearly 24 hours a day with His disciples. That is nearly 27,000 hours! We can never hope to mimic that, but discipleship isn't just about an hour of formal Bible study a week. The best discipleship involves a disciple being able to see us in action: how we handle pressure and reach out to others, how we handle a relationship problem and how we serve the church. You'd be amazed what someone can learn by watching us and glimpsing our attitudes. Much of discipleship is just 'hanging around' together and discussing issues as they come up.

I have had short-term mission teams live with me for several weeks. Although crowded, I choose to do this because the discipling benefits far outweigh the disadvantages. I have also been able to have apprentices live with me for up to a year at a time. A much more informal kind of discipling takes place during these times. The short-term teams and apprentices learn about being a Christian by seeing me live out my Christian life in simple tasks like doing housework and seeing how I set boundaries to ensure holiness in my life. They also see my many faults and learn something of what it means to be a flawed and sinful human being. There are also opportunities for lots of informal discussions related to books they're reading and things they're thinking about.

Married people must remember their prime responsibility is to disciple their own spouse and children. Years of living together will have a big impact. Will it lead each family member to know God better and grow in godliness, or will it result in a total rejection of you and the God you serve?

We live so separately from others now, but we could make such an impact if we just took others along on the things we were doing – that is, if we are worth being followed! How much a young single man or woman could learn if a Christian family adopted them and invited them often for meals and family outings.

Reflection:

1. What did Jesus pray for the disciples (and us) in John 17?
2. Write down a list of what you think you should be praying for a specific disciple and then pray.
3. What are some things you do that you could invite your disciple to accompany you to? What are potential things they could learn? What questions could you ask that might help them learn even more?

6: Should I be Involved in Discipling?

What does God want you to be involved in?

Often we drift into things because we don't really pray or set priorities. At the very least, once a year we should set aside some time for reflection on the previous year and asking God for guidance on the coming year. If we are to live our lives as God wants and bring Him glory, this kind of reflection and prayer is essential. Perhaps we think this kind of practice is only for full-time paid ministry professionals (for want of a better term), but the Bible doesn't make that sort of distinction. All are regarded equally as 'salt' and 'light' (Matt. 5:13-16) in their communities and with our eternal purpose to bring God the honour He deserves. I find that impossible to do without times of prayer and reflection. Interestingly, adding that time into my life helps me perceive my priorities and I'm able to cut a lot of things out of my life that might be 'good' but aren't the best.

A friend of mine noted recently, 'Christians have become so busy that even when a wonderful opportunity to talk with a non-Christian (or Christian) comes up, it is regarded more as a tragedy than a blessing!' How can we be going so wrong that people who need ministry and encouragement and the gospel can be regarded as a disaster messing up our plans?

Are you involved in other ministries?
Most churches have a full range of children's programmes, youth groups, Bible studies and other activities. All of these need leaders and there can be pressure to be involved. A Christian declining to be involved because they want to personally disciple others can be misunderstood. The time has perhaps come for the church to ask itself if it is really discipling its members by the current methods. Are all the programmes necessary? Are there things which could be cut or adapted to make sure people really are growing to maturity?

The decision to be involved in discipling is seldom applauded, simply because it is a background ministry, hidden from others because it occurs one-to-one. We naturally desire human praise and that can drive us to be involved in up-front ministries. It takes great courage to persevere in a ministry unseen by human eyes. Can we dare to be unseen for the sake of God's Kingdom? Discipling does have very great rewards in terms of joy and satisfaction, but those rewards only come some months after you've dared to start.

Do you have the time?
Many Christians work or study full-time and have a plethora of other responsibilities as well. Participating in one service a week and a Bible study group may be as much as they can cope with. People with children need to dedicate time to their children's growth and church events, missing out on their own groups for the sake of their children. Where would someone like this find the time in an already packed schedule to disciple another? As it is, they struggle to even do personal Bible study and prayer.

A friend I'm currently discipling suggested that it is easier to just let the church organize us into Bible study groups because that is more passive. Discipling requires us to take the initiative to find someone to disciple and spend time in preparation. For many, that is just too much effort.

Are you worried you don't know how to disciple?

Very few of us have ever been discipled ourselves and so we either don't even think about this ministry or we lack the confidence to start. The good news is that the Bible has guidelines to show us how and some practical things we will only discover by trial and error. This book is written for all those who are not self-starters and who have wondered, as I did, what Jesus meant by 'make disciples'.

Are you afraid?

This is the major reason that we avoid doing many things that God would like us to. We fear that we'll do a bad job and not only fail but hurt someone else at the same time. We fear that our lives aren't worth imitating and that discipling someone else will reveal us as a fraud. We also may have very big fears related to the personal nature of one-to-one ministry. We are afraid of getting to know someone to the level where our failures and flaws will be seen.

Fear is one of Satan's most successful weapons and it successfully keeps many Christians from maturing. We need to choose to trust God, that He will give us all the resources we need. After all, His commission to us in Matthew 28 promised that He would. Many of us are willing to say 'God is all-powerful', but content not to put it to the test. The way to maturity is to take God at His word and launch off the cliff. God's 'wings' are fully reliable; there is no reason to fear at all.

Are you worth following?

Many of us feel that we hardly qualify to be called 'mature'. We might feel that it is quite arrogant to even feel that we could disciple another person.

Let's look again at Jesus' last command to his disciples:

> 'All authority in heaven and on earth has been given to me. Therefore go and make disciples of all nations, baptizing them in the name of the Father and the Son and the Holy Spirit and teaching them to obey all I have commanded you. And surely I am with you even to the end of the age' (Matt. 28:18-20).

41

Did Jesus qualify this statement by saying, 'when you have reached a certain maturity, then you have earned the right to be involved in discipling others'? We need to remember whom Jesus was talking to. How mature were they? Judging by their behaviour they still had a long way to go. Only weeks before, they'd all abandoned Jesus and Peter denied Him vehemently.

The verses above contain the clue. We disciple not because we are especially mature or competent, but because Jesus commands us to make this our priority. We are able to do so because Jesus gives us all the resources we need. Yes, we lack wisdom and discernment. Yes, we often feel overwhelmed and stupid. Unfortunately there are some areas in my life that I don't want those I disciple to imitate. But we have all of God's resources, His wisdom, love and knowledge, at our disposal. Jesus didn't tell the disciples to wait until they were perfect before they started discipling others. Part of God's amazing plan is that He chooses to work through us in our imperfect state. Amazing, isn't it? Over and over Christians who trust God will be amazed by the words that they hear themselves speak in tough situations. Our wisdom is limited but God graciously speaks His wisdom through us.

There is another clue in the passage. Teaching others is not based on our authority but Jesus'. A fatal mistake is to ever think that it is our authority that matters. That is the way into the dangers of pride, frustration and failure. Don't let people quote you, or your books, or ideas. Our attitude must be 'He must increase and I must decrease' (John 3:30 ESV). Our words are irrelevant. What we should emphasize is, 'what does God say in His Word?' Be wary when Christians constantly quote someone else. People's words only have value where they reflect the Bible. Humans are so frail and sinful; I would hate to make people 'my' disciples. It is Jesus I want them to follow, not me!

People I disciple might think I am very pedantic on this point. I don't like people saying, 'I think' but will often say, 'Yes, but what does the BIBLE say?' It is the Bible that is our only authority.

There are great dangers in having any other standards. If we stick to the Bible we're safe. The Bible has all the answers to every problem, and counselling only has value if it reflects God's truth.

This issue of 'what is the authority?' becomes very important when we are rebuking or challenging someone. If we have set up ourselves as the authority (implicitly or explicitly), then we shouldn't be surprised if the person says, 'So what!' However, if we have done our job of setting up God and His Word as the sole authority, then it is very hard to argue with that as you find yourself arguing against the King of the universe.

In conclusion, discipling others is not only a task for those who are spiritual giants. Jesus commanded us all to be involved and reminded us to trust Him because He is the source of all the resources we need. Discipling others is like passing on a baton in a relay race. We take God's Word and pass it on to the next runner (2 Tim. 2:2). Discipling is a privilege and not something to be feared or treated lightly. What we are entrusted with are the very words of God. It is a sacred task. An awesome privilege and responsibility.

Take the discipling challenge. Choose to disciple one person this year and then reassess. I will be surprised if you don't get excited about this kind of ministry.

Reflection:

1. Do you have other reasons for not being involved in discipling? What are they?
2. Spend some time (at least one hour) in prayer and reflection asking God to help you set priorities for this year.
3. What are you afraid of? How does this chapter help you?
4. What is your view of the Bible and its importance?
5. What are the dangers to us as the discipler, the disciple and others at church of the constant repetition of the phrase 'X (your name) says'?
6. Can you think of more safeguards to protect ourselves from becoming the authority?

PART TWO:
THE
PRACTICALITIES
OF
DISCIPLING

7: Who Should I Disciple?

The simple answer is everyone! Everyone could benefit from discipleship, but the reality is that we don't have time to do so and we may not be a suitable discipler for everyone we meet. How then do we choose?

I was already 26 when I formally discipled someone for the first time. I'd been on an overseas trip to visit some missionaries and during that time God laid the burden of discipleship on my heart. I prayed and asked God whom I should spend my time with and He guided me towards one person. I was going into Bible College and knew that my time would be limited and so I prayed that if God really wanted me to disciple that person, He would make it clear to me. About a week after I arrived home the young lady came and spoke to me and asked if I would disciple her. That was all the confirmation I needed.

Principle 1: Pray First

The Gospels say that Jesus prayed all night before choosing His twelve disciples. Most people will only be able to disciple one or two people a year. It makes sense not to hurry into that decision. I often think of someone and then pray for several months before I approach them.

Principle 2: God's Timing Is Always Perfect

Sometimes when I ask someone if they would like to be discipled, they joyfully reply, 'I'd love that and was thinking about it too, but was too shy to ask.' At other times I get the timing wrong and it is months or even a year later that they get back to me and ask if the offer is still open. Don't worry about getting the 'right time'; God's timing may be different to ours, but it is always perfect.

Principle 3: Choose Someone Who Desires To Grow

Disciples need to want to grow and learn. If they're agreeing to do discipleship because they think they ought to, or out of a sense of obligation, they'll nearly always drop out along the way. Remember, though, that some who show no outward desire to grow may be the ones who desperately need to. Do not dismiss someone because they may be difficult to disciple.

Principle 4: Create Hunger

There are many people to whom the whole concept of discipleship is so strange and even frightening that they may appear uninterested. Fear is common when people face the unfamiliar. Many guess that one-to-one Bible study could be quite intense and they fear that they will be exposed. People often need to be reassured and challenged to try a week or two. After that they usually grow enthusiastic. However, if they don't, then there would be nothing wrong with agreeing not to continue. Perhaps we were the wrong person to disciple them or the timing wasn't right.

Dana was someone with whom I aimed to create hunger. We got to know each other as she helped me practise reading Chinese newspapers. In one of the early weeks I asked,

'How long have you been a Christian?'

'About 15 years.'

'Are your parents and siblings Christians?'

'No.'

'How does this make you feel?'

Dana didn't understand my question, I tried again, 'Does it bother you that your family don't know Jesus and are not headed for heaven?'

'No.'

It would have been easy to think this woman was not even a Christian, but I had learnt not to judge too quickly. It turned out that she had no concern for her family's eternal situation because her own spiritual life was just a spark. No one had ever taught her to study the Bible for herself. Weekly sermons and adult Bible classes mostly went over her head and were totally unrelated to her everyday life.

Whether Dana had been a non-Christian or not, I still would have followed the same course of action. We started doing a simple Old Testament overview designed to help her see the overall picture of the Bible so that she could better understand why Jesus had to come and how He saved us. I didn't even raise the issue of evangelism or her parents' situation. I was convinced that if she grew to love Jesus, she wouldn't be able to keep Him to herself. Within six weeks she was on the way to being a different person. Soon after, she invited her parents to church, and by the end of the year her very traditional Chinese 80-year-old father was baptized. It all started with creating spiritual hunger in one lady, who then got excited about Jesus and passed it on.

Another group of people who might not seem interested in discipleship are the ones who are so needy that they can see nothing but their own problems. What they want is for someone to sit and listen and then tell them that they have a terrible life. You could sit there for a year listening like this, but are unlikely to see any change or growth at all. I have spent a lot of time with depressed people. It is tempting to let them dominate every session. There are times to just listen, but it is as we learn God's views of life and our problems that there is growth.

Sue was a young mother who worked full-time as a shift-work nurse. She had a range of problems in her life and it was not too surprising that she ended up depressed. She was on the appropriate anti-depressant medication, but then the hard work starts – the battle for the mind. She was not really interested in studying the Bible, but all the listening and counselling in the world would never change her life. Only God could do that and He chooses to do it through His Word.

Sue wasn't sleeping well, and so we limited our time and studied one paragraph at a time of Luke. I think she was pretty dubious that what she perceived as 'my method' would work. She was surprised to discover how God seemed to know just what she needed to hear, and each time the passage applied to her. I just followed through in the order it was written, so God was choosing the passages, not me. So often when we choose the topic we get it wrong or misinterpret the passages to suit ourselves. There was a rapid improvement in Sue's depression and spiritual growth as she applied the Bible to her life. She learnt to refuse to listen to Satan's lies and to remind herself of truth.

Principle 5: Remember the Ones Others Forget

People who are not so eager or are shy, less intelligent, disabled or less like ourselves are often forgotten in discipling. We often have a worldly way of choosing disciples based more on those who will make us look good.

I remember one unprepossessing lady who was so shy that she kept her head lowered most of the time. She found study hard and would often attend my adult Bible study twice so she could get more out of it. She never answered questions or came up with anything brilliant. She had no apparent spiritual gifts. She worked at the local post-office but had always been too shy and lacking in confidence to share about Jesus with her workmates. She wanted to learn and willingly served others by humbly sweeping and cleaning up, but I was concerned about her because her husband was studying to be a pastor. Knowing the pressures for pastors' wives, I thought she would really struggle. This lady was so much in the background that it took a while for God to help me notice her.

So I asked if we could study Ephesians together. From the first she was hungry to learn and started to open up, but it was while talking about what it means practically to 'use the sword of the Spirit, which is the Word of God' (Eph. 6:17) that the breakthrough came. I chose to apply the idea to the issue of low self-esteem and fear. We wrote down all sorts of verses and biblical ideas related to these issues. For homework I asked her to read through the verses morning and night. The first week she forgot. This was unusual. The second week was the same and I began to be suspicious. I knew these issues were important and preventing her spiritual growth. It seemed to me that Satan was the most likely cause of her unusual forgetfulness. So I devised other ways to remind her. The third week there was a noticeable difference in her.

Soon the constant repetition of Scripture changed her self-perception. Her head came up and she stopped stooping. Reciting verses to do with fear reminded her how God was with her and could be relied upon. Soon after, she started sharing about Jesus at work, and within six months had led her first friends to Christ.

Principle 6: Same Gender

Reading the above stories may give you a glimpse of the intimacy of discipling. We need to consider the implications of forming such an intimate relationship and take suitable steps to avoid any complications. These are the guidelines I follow myself. I offer them as something to think about:

Never meet alone with someone of the opposite sex for Bible study. We need to be aware of human weakness. In addition, neighbours can so easily draw the wrong conclusions. Once they've opened their mouths, even with a lie, there is very little protection for us. A good name once lost is often lost forever.

I once surprised a 15-year-old student because I wouldn't have him in my home for an hour but insisted on sitting outside a friend's house. I was protecting my reputation and the good name of Jesus who mustn't be associated with even the suspicion of impurity.

If for some reason you need to meet a member of the opposite sex for a short time, maybe because you are the only Christian they know for example, then always make sure it is in a group of three – disciple couples together for example, or ask two friends to come together.

Principle 7: Age
There are many different opinions and preferences, but generally there is no age barrier. Perhaps, when starting out, we should meet people the same age or younger than us, but as we gain experience, age matters less and less. The key to meeting someone is our attitude. If we ever communicate, 'I know it all and am more spiritually mature than you', then I'd be surprised if anyone wants to meet you. Our attitude needs to be along the lines of 'we are two fellow pilgrims on God's road, helping each other and growing together'.

Let me plead especially for men to be involved in discipling others. If men won't disciple others, then the women will continue to be more mature and the church will remain as skewed as it is in many countries (some churches are 90 per cent women).

Principle 8: Take Your Time
You don't need to rush into anything. Spend some weeks praying about those you could possibly disciple. Take time to talk to the person themselves and see if they want to be discipled. It is no use forcing someone. Why not set up a first session to meet them when you can both check each other out, making it clear that either of you can back out after that? Or why not just try to meet for a specific number of weeks with the option to rethink the relationship after that? Don't be afraid to recommend they meet someone else who suits them better.

One of my worst discipleship experiences was with a couple of young ladies who had no desire to be discipled, but I foolishly persisted. One of the best was a request from a friend to disciple an overseas student from Mongolia. I agreed to meet for an initial assessment session. It was immediately obvious that she was someone who was eager to learn. What an amazing privilege it was to disciple her that year. She returned to Mongolia and continues to have a wide impact, bringing many to Christ and discipling others.

Who Did Jesus Choose?

Jesus did not choose those whom we would choose.

If it had been me, I'm sure I would have chosen people with more education (a lawyer or two to deal with tough questions), more influence and political connections (a few religious leaders would have been useful to hopefully defuse some of their opposition to Jesus and give an appearance of respectability), more money (a rich supporter so we wouldn't have to worry about food or accommodation). I would probably have chosen only people who looked respectable and perhaps I would have taken some women or some from minority groups for political correctness. But Jesus chose the most unlikely people: a fisherman (not much education and probably lots of brawn and bad language), a tax collector (viewed as the lowest of the low and traitors to their own country), some brothers famous for their hot tempers, and of course Judas, whom Jesus knew would betray Him (John 6:71). We don't know much about the rest except they were unlikely to be special in society's view.

Jesus did not choose His disciples in a hurry. He first chose Peter, Andrew, James and John and then later Levi (Mark 1:16-20, 2:13ff). After spending a night in prayer (Luke 6:12) He then chose the final few.

Reflection:

1. Look again at all the principles. Can you think of some possible people you could disciple? Start praying about

them. Are you simply choosing 'easy' people who are like yourself, or people whom God wants you to disciple?

8: How to Disciple

I hesitate to even write something about how to disciple. Some people will be tempted to try to make the principles in this book into rigid steps. That will only lead to frustration. This book aims to give you principles and suggestions so that you have the basics from which you can make decisions to suit the individuals you disciple. The key word in one-to-one discipleship is flexibility. Discipleship is an art not a science. It is not about doing the same thing each time, in the same order and producing the same result. It is about relying on the Holy Spirit to help you teach and model so that each person grows to maturity.

But being flexible is hard work. Many of us feel much safer if we are in control and following a recipe with a set series of steps. Paul's words in 1 Corinthians are an important corrective: 'To the Jews, I became like a Jew, to win the Jews…to those not having the law, I became like one not having the law…so as to win those not having the law … to the weak I became weak, to win the weak. I have become all things to all men so that by all possible means I might save some' (1 Cor. 9:20-22). In other words, Paul was willing to adapt himself in any way to make the other person more comfortable and better able to understand what was being communicated. He never demanded that the other person first became like him in order that they might hear the gospel. Paul was clear on his goal: to share the gospel and to 'present everyone complete in Christ' (Col. 1:28 NASB).

THE FIRST SESSION

Your first discipleship session should be designed to:

1) Start establishing trust;
2) Start getting to know each other at a deeper level;
3) Start working out where the disciple is at spiritually and what you will do in subsequent discipleship sessions.

How are you going to achieve this?

Thinking About Where and When

Jesus was flexible and seized opportunities anywhere to teach spiritual truth.

Jesus' disciples spent much time with Him, following Him as He went about His business. As such, He seized opportunities to teach them whenever they arose and did not wait for formal times of study. No time was wasted. For example, in the temple courtyards Jesus drew the disciples' attention to the widow's offering and so taught them about the right attitude for making offerings to God (Luke 21:1-4). The disciples were also there when Jesus overturned the tables and threw the sellers out of the temple (Luke 19:45ff). Much of Jesus' teaching was done on the mountain or roadside. His disciples were fishermen and felt comfortable out in their boats. Jesus took this opportunity to spend time with them and teach them lessons from the environment they were familiar with. In the boat they watched Jesus calm the storm and walk on water (Mark 4:35ff, 6:45ff). Jesus was also able to teach by letting the disciples see who He spent time with – eating in the homes of sinners challenged the disciples' thinking (Luke 19:1-10).

Jesus also was never too self-absorbed to teach and was ready to make a lesson out of every event. Even on the cross He was able to disciple and exemplify how to care for others. Despite His physical pain and mental anguish, He ministered to the repentant thief and to John and His mother (Luke 23:32ff; John 19:25-27).

Jesus did teach large crowds and would speak in the synagogue, but He used this period of formal teaching to then draw aside with His disciples and give them further explanation.

Where?

Imagine a situation in which you are discipling a married couple. It is convenient for you to meet them at 1pm. You meet in a restaurant that has a TV on in one corner. You have to sit facing it. Next to the table is a comfy chair where the wife, exhausted by a sleepless night, sits. People pass to and from the table, a telephone rings constantly and other people try to conceal their curiosity in whatever you are doing. You've chosen a passage to study and press doggedly on despite the situation.

We can all see the obvious problems with the situation above. Here are some principles to consider when deciding where to meet:

1. *Minimize distractions*

Satan is never keen for us to study the Bible. He'll use any means at his disposal and often we really help him out by our choices. In the above example, there were many different distractions – the TV, the telephone ringing, people passing the table and the restaurant that is not designed for uninterrupted meetings. The chance of this couple even hearing anything is minimal, let alone remembering it.

We need to choose a place where we can be quiet and concentrate. Meeting in someone's house may seem like a good idea, but if they have children or pets, or constantly have the TV on or the phone ringing, then this setting will be no better than the overcrowded restaurant.

2. *Maximize eye contact*

In the above example, the wife was sitting separately to the other two. Being in a comfortable chair, her eyes were probably at a lower level and tilted back. It is important that all our eyes are level and able to see each other. That helps us to relate well and will really help communication.

3. Maximize chances of staying awake

The wife probably fell asleep in the above example. She was already tired and sat in a sleep-inducing chair. Straight-backed chairs are much better. They don't have to be uncomfortable but just something that helps people concentrate.

4. Maximize the disciple's feeling of security

Perhaps meet in the person's house but remember to think about their situation. A mother with young children might be able to arrange for someone else to look after the children and is pleased for a chance to get out of the house. Someone who is the only Christian in the family might not want to be doing Bible study under the eyes of the rest of the family. Actually this situation is a good one to discuss as sometimes such a thing would be very helpful for the non-Christian family. It all depends on their attitude to Christians. I have often deliberately chosen to do discipleship in the home where there are a majority of non-Christians so that we might have the opportunity to make an impact on them. Sometimes, however, this would simply provoke them. The aim is always to help the disciple and their family move towards knowing Jesus.

Using your own house makes it easier to control interruptions, where you can take the phone off the hook and ensure that there is minimal noise. It also allows us to model Christian hospitality.

Sometimes a neutral place is best. I've used cafés (quiet ones and in their less busy times) and parks. Use your imagination to add variety to your meetings.

5. Maximize convenience

You might choose a place midway between your homes so that both have less travel. Or you might alternate homes for the same reason. On the way back from work might also be easy. The main point is that you do not want it to be a burden for the individual to get there. The discipline of discipleship is already hard enough without giving any more reasons for them to give up. There are many options, so use your imagination to maximize your useful time together.

6. *Decent lighting*
This tends to be something you don't notice unless you don't have it. A warm, relaxed atmosphere can be achieved by the kind of lighting you choose. Again, the lighting should be such as to maximise our ability to read God's Word and feel relaxed.

7. *Food and drink*
Having a drink and a few snacks can make the person feel more relaxed and comfortable. Why not invite the disciple to have a meal with you and use the time to chat informally before starting the Bible study?

8. *Maximize opportunities!*
I include this principle just to remind us that discipleship isn't just about a one-to-one formal meeting once a week. True discipleship is about sharing our lives. Any situation or time can be part of the process. It is important to realize that our discipleship doesn't end with one hour of Bible study a week.

When?
Choosing a suitable time to meet is vitally important. Trying to squeeze discipleship in between other activities will leave the person we are meeting feeling unvalued and a burden to us. Choosing a time when we are tired or preoccupied will also not help us get the most out of the study. Here are some principles to consider while deciding when to meet:

1. *When you are most alert*
Some of us are more alert in the morning and others in the evening. Be willing to sacrifice yourself in this area. If we're a 'night owl', this sacrifice might mean going to bed early the

night before a 6 a.m. discipleship session with a businessperson who only has that time free.

2. *Their convenience*
Choose a time suitable for them. It is wise not to fill up your entire schedule, leaving them only one possible slot. Be prepared to be flexible with your time.

3. *Always be flexible*
For various reasons sudden changes may need to be made, especially when dealing with those on shiftwork or mothers with young children. Try to schedule in a basic time and ask them to let you know if that time needs to be changed as soon as they can. It is important to encourage a consideration of others.

4. *Make the scheduled time a priority*
Both parties need to respect each other. Such things as leaving your mobile phone switched on or being late quickly show the other person that discipleship is not a priority.

Opening Each Session
People in any culture do not respond well to immediately jumping to business. Discipleship is much the same. If the minute someone walks into the room we say, 'Open your Bible and let's begin', it will seem very abrupt. People want to know that we care about them and not just our own programme. Each time the disciple and discipler get together, it is about far more than following a rigid plan. The whole point of discipleship is that it is growth in the context of a relationship. Open each session with general conversation, offering them a drink and praying before you begin. Starting with a question like 'what has God been teaching you this week?' or 'what challenges have you faced this week?' eases us into the formal study time. Do make sure you don't just end up spending the whole session chatting!

Reflection:

1. What are some questions that you could ask at the beginning of your first session with a new disciple that would help you get to know each other and clarify expectations?
2. Choose three different people and think through what setting/atmosphere/timing would make them feel most at ease.

9: Spiritual Diagnosis

Normal Growth Patterns

When I was studying physiotherapy we spent a lot of time studying the normal growth and movement patterns of humans. Sometimes this seemed a waste of time because we longed to get on to learning about the far more interesting, abnormal conditions. However, our teachers knew that if we recognized normal, we'd always be able to quickly recognize anything that was abnormal.

Christian growth is much the same. If we are aware of what is 'normal' in Christian growth, then we will not only more easily recognize problems but we will have more patience with people. We often have unrealistic expectations. After all, would we expect a baby to feed and dress itself? God has taken over thirty years to mature me to my current stage and I have had excellent Christian parents and a lifetime of good Bible teaching. Maturing as a Christian is a lifelong process but God promises that He will carry it on to completion (Phil. 1:6) so that we will be transformed into His likeness with ever increasing glory (2 Cor. 3:18).

General Principles

A patient comes to their doctor complaining of pain. The doctor will ask lots of questions, do a physical examination and send the patient for further tests. The goal is to end up with an accurate diagnosis. This is essential if the treatment is to be effective. Spiritual diagnosis is a similar skill, and, like doctors, our ability to diagnose spiritual ills will improve with practice.

Let's start with a biblical example. Have the diagrams of the 'links in the chain' and 'brick wall' from chapter four drawn on two pieces of paper, ready to do some spiritual diagnosis on King Nebuchadnezzar.

King Nebuchadnezzar was king during the golden years of the Babylonian empire. Babylon (modern Iraq) expanded into the area held by the Assyrian empire about 600 B.C. Under Nebuchadnezzar the empire expanded to include the areas to the north in Asia Minor (now Turkey) and west nearly to Egypt. He also conquered the southern Kingdom of Judah. In 587 B.C. many of the people of Jerusalem, especially the wealthy and educated, were transported to Babylon. One of those young noblemen was Daniel. Nebuchadnezzar's policy was to choose the most intelligent and educate them at the best university. The top graduates then became the king's officials. It seemed like an excellent opportunity for Daniel, but it set up a crisis for him. The Babylonians worshipped many different gods and at university Daniel faced temptation to forget or compromise his beliefs. He chose to wholeheartedly follow God no matter what it cost him. Daniel would be the means that God could use to teach King Nebuchadnezzar about Himself.[1]

1. Look at Daniel 2:1-10 and 2 Chronicles 32:10-15 and try to identify the 'bricks' in King Nebuchadnezzar's thinking before he knew anything about the God of the Bible. N.B. 2 Chronicles is not about Nebuchadnezzar himself, but his thinking would have been similar.

2. Identify where you would place the king on the 'links in the chain' diagram. There is no need to be precise.

Now read all of Daniel 2-3, noting what God teaches Nebuchadnezzar about who God is. Then especially look at 2:46-49 and 3:1, 28-30.

---

1 Answers can be found in Appendix A on p. 141.

3. Is there any evidence that the king has become a believer?

4. Where might you place Nebuchadnezzar on the 'links in the chain' diagram now?

At this point in spiritual diagnosis it is useful to understand what kind of evidence you would expect to see in a believer. Jesus used a very simple illustration; He talked about the tree and its fruit.

> 'Every good tree bears good fruit, but a bad tree bears bad fruit. A good tree cannot bear bad fruit and a bad tree cannot bear good fruit ... by their fruit will you recognize them' (Matt. 7:17-20).

A Christian should produce fruit (i.e. attitudes, values and actions) in line with their new situation. If we don't have God's life in us then it will be increasingly obvious. People might fool us for a while but eventually they won't be able to maintain the act. Under pressure the real person will be revealed. Paul lists some examples of good and bad fruit by which we should be able to distinguish believers from non-believers (Gal. 5:19-22). The 'fruit' of the sinful nature includes sexual immorality and impurity, idolatry and witchcraft, hatred, discord, jealousy, fits of rage, selfish ambition, dissensions and factions, envy, drunkenness and orgies. Not a very pleasant-sounding list. Maybe it describes your office! The fruit of the Spirit are listed as love, joy, peace, patience, kindness, goodness, faithfulness, gentleness and self-control. Christians will never be completely perfect but they should be much more like the good fruit than the bad fruit.

Now read all of Daniel 4.

5. What is the real issue in Nebuchadnezzar's life (v. 30-32)?

Now read verses 1-3 and 34-37.

6. Is there enough evidence to show that Nebuchadnezzar is a believer?

Spiritual Diagnosis Questions

Asking questions is an art. The first thing to understand is that there are many different kinds of questions. Questions that only require a short answer and don't lead to further discussion are called closed questions. Open questions lead to further discussion and often use words like 'how', 'why', 'describe', 'evaluate' and 'explain'.

Some good questions to use are listed below. These start from questions designed to see if someone is a Christian and then progress. There are as many questions as there are ways to ask them. As you experiment you will discover that sometimes your questions are too direct and you need to find a better way of asking them.

- What do you think is wrong with the world?
- What do you think is the solution?
- Who do you think Jesus is? Or what do you know about Jesus?
- What do you believe about life after death?
- How do you think someone gets into heaven?
- How would you explain to someone what a Christian is?

This one question allows me to see if they are clear themselves and might give me a hint whether in fact they are a Christian (be careful – some people aren't good at explaining but they may in fact be a Christian).

- What are some of the benefits of being a Christian?
- What changes have you seen in your life?
- What issues do you still struggle with?

Some cautions

- Be very careful of your tone of voice. If people seem to react badly to your questions, for example by getting angry or trying to change the subject, then tone of voice is often the culprit. Ask a friend some questions and get them to tell you how they feel and why, and ask for help. Discipleship is not an inquisition, and we must not assume we know where someone is at in their spiritual journey and let that affect how we relate to them.
- Be careful not to seem to be 'making judgments'. If a person knows your questions are aimed at helping you

to get to know and be better able to serve them, they'll be more relaxed.

- Always be prepared to revise your diagnosis. Remember it is provisional.
- Beware of pride. We do diagnosis to help us better know what is appropriate to share or study with someone, not to feel superior. We need to constantly remind ourselves that discipleship is not about a superior-inferior relationship. Yes, we may be further along the road than the person we disciple, but that is because of Christ's grace not our own greatness.

Reflection:

Here are some further case studies. For each case consider what any 'bricks' might be, assess where the person might be spiritually, using the 'chain' diagram, and think through what questions you could ask to make the diagnosis more accurate.[27]

Case Study 1:

I met Julie, a lady in her 20s, in church. I asked her if she was a Christian and she said, 'I haven't been baptized yet.' This is a particularly common scenario in Taiwan where I work.

Case Study 2:

Esther is in her 40s and grew up in a family that became Christian when she was a teenager. She was baptized along with her two sisters and parents. Later she married a non-Christian. Her older sister, who was a keen Christian, introduced us in the hope that I would do Bible study with Esther. This I did. Esther also started coming to church every week.

Case Study 3:

A man I met in a non-Christian setting quickly told me he was a Roman Catholic who went to Mass each week.

---

2   Answers can be found in Appendix B on p. 143.

Case Study 4:
Caroline came to faith a year ago. Her husband came to faith shortly after her. Now the whole family attend a house church in their town. One day, you go to visit them and learn that Caroline is gone. Their youngest child is sick and she has taken him to a faith healer.

Case Study 5:
John, his wife and five children are active in a Catholic charismatic group. At one of the meetings, they seem to have come to faith in Jesus. As a result, John destroyed their idols. He now feels sure that he will go to heaven since he has not committed a major sin.

Case Study 6:
A couple married a year ago and live in the husband's parents' house. A colleague led the wife, Rachel, to faith and then Rachel led her husband to faith. They attended a Bible-teaching church for a month. They stopped, though, because his mother threatened to kick them out of the house.

10: STUDYING THE BIBLE

An important responsibility in discipleship is to teach others to know God's Word, to study it for themselves and to be able to correctly apply it to their lives. Every Christian is given the Holy Spirit as a gift at conversion. A large part of the Holy Spirit's role is to help us understand God's Word, and through that Word to challenge and convict us. As a discipler, we need to teach the individual to read the Scripture and trust the Holy Spirit to help them understand it. They'll often want us to give them the answers but it will be far better for their maturity if we point them to the appropriate Bible passages rather than just feeding them the answers.

Before Jesus started His official ministry He went through a time of difficult preparation. Really God had already been preparing Him for about 30 years and Jesus completes His preparation with 40 days of fasting in the desert. Just when Jesus is at His weakest, Satan arrives to try to tempt Him away from His life's purpose. Three times Satan tempts Jesus to use His powers for Himself and to honour someone other than God the Father. The temptations might seem at first glance to be fairly innocuous. After all what would have been so wrong for a very hungry Jesus to turn stones into bread? He could have argued that it was a good thing to do to give Him the energy He needed to serve God. Satan was very clever and knew that if Jesus ever acted independently of God, then He would have rebelled as surely as the greatest criminal. Jesus must stick to God's way, or He could not save the world. Setting aside issues of the Trinity, it is very interesting to see how Jesus answered Satan each of the three times. Jesus was God Himself and had God's authority. He could have just used His own words to answer Satan. But He doesn't. Each of the three times He quotes from the Bible. He gives us the model that in every situation, the Bible is to be our only authority. If Jesus Himself relied on the Bible as His authority, how can we do otherwise?

Let me summarize what the Bible claims about itself and Jesus supported:

1. The Bible is God's Word (Matt. 19:3ff, John 10:34-35);
2. The Bible is 100% true (Matt. 5:18, 2 Tim. 3:16-17, 2 Pet. 1:16-21);
3. The Bible is our weapon against Satan (Luke 4:1-13; Eph. 6:17).

Through the ages, many have exploited the phrase 'the Bible says' to justify such atrocities as slavery, polygamy, war and authoritarian leadership. These examples show us the importance of studying the Bible for ourselves and studying it in an appropriate way. Here are some tips for correctly studying the Bible:

1. Study all passages in context. Studying whole books of the Bible is a helpful safeguard.
2. Next to answers, note the verse from which you've taken them. Noting the verse allows others to say, 'I don't see that!' and helps us be corrected if necessary.
3. No one is above being asked 'where do you find that idea?' or being disagreed with.
4. Have an attitude of always learning and acknowledging by apology when you get something wrong.

5. Allow the Bible to change your ideas. If something we hold dear is not in the Bible then we need to correct our thinking to be in line with what God says.

Choosing What to Study
Before making a decision about what to study, we need to think through the following issues:

- Where is the individual spiritually?
  We need to make sure we are targeting the individual's needs and making the Scripture applicable to their lives. To do this we need to know where they are.

- What do they already know and which books of the Bible have they already read?
  Some form of Bible overview is a good general starting place, providing a skeleton for the individual to base further knowledge around. Studying a Gospel ensures you are starting from a solid foundation.

- Which books and topics are we familiar with?
  At the beginning there might be books of the Bible that we don't have the confidence to tackle. Start with something you feel more familiar with.

- How long will we be meeting for?
  If you only have a few weeks to meet in, then choose a shorter book you can complete in the time. In general each course of study shouldn't be longer than about six to eight weeks. People tend to like some change after this time. Watch their interest levels. Don't allow a course of Bible study to drag on.

- What happens if we're studying a long book of the Bible?
  There are various options. You could just choose a few key chapters that give the overall flow of the book, or you could study eight weeks and then have a break and

come back to the next section. Another option would be to follow one main theme through a book, then come back to another theme later. With historical books like 1 and 2 Samuel, for example, that have several main characters you could study first Samuel, then Saul and then David. A good conclusion could be to compare and contrast them.

Again, the key is flexibility. Disciples are unique and will all find different things helpful. Continually review how things are going and ask your disciple what they have found helpful.

SOME GENERAL GUIDELINES FOR DISCIPLING CHRISTIANS AT DIFFERENT LEVELS OF MATURITY

New Christians

New Christians will have varying levels of knowledge but most won't be familiar with the Bible. They may even fear it as it seems a thick book and often looks like it will be difficult to understand – the often black binding, formal print and column layout is rather different from most novels! New Christians may struggle to find their way around the Bible and not even be aware that the Bible isn't just one book. They might not even know about chapters and verses and how those are annotated.

Everything is new to them. Suddenly the whole foundation of their life has shifted. This may be exciting but is also rather daunting. It is similar to the experience I had when I became a missionary. Suddenly, as a 29-year-old, I couldn't communicate and couldn't even read the street or shop signs. It was a horrible experience to feel so out of control. Becoming a Christian is similar, especially when the new believer has come from a culture completely at odds with the Christian culture. Imagine what it must feel like to become a Christian from an idol-worshipping or a Muslim background. What about someone who has become a Christian just out of jail or from a background of broken homes, drugs and violence?

Let me share the story of one new Christian:

A short-term mission team came to teach English in Taiwan. One of the adults who attended the class was Grandpa Wu. He was soon chatting to a member of the team who could speak Chinese.

Grandpa Wu shared his difficulties about raising his grandchildren and about his son who had dropped out of school and was unemployed. Hearing of a God who loved him, Grandpa Wu accepted God's gift of salvation with joy.

Not long after, the short-term workers left and there was no one to follow up Grandpa Wu. Grandpa knew that Christians go to church and so he arranged to go. Asked later how it went, Grandpa looked very downcast: 'I didn't know what they were talking about! They stood up and sat down and read from this big book full of hard words and they turned pages all over the place'[1].

We need to put ourselves in the new Christian's shoes and think through carefully what we are going to teach. Consider looking at some of the following:

- Practical skills such as how to study the Bible, how to pray and how to share the gospel with others.
- A Bible overview, relating the Old Testament to the New, covering topics such as the Passover, that will help the disciple understand the concepts of the New Testament.
- A Gospel, to ensure they have understood the basics. If they've already studied one Gospel, I might choose to do John with them as it has a different style to the other three Gospels.
- Acts, as it deals with lots of issues related to the church and how God works.
- A Pauline letter – Ephesians is helpful as it covers the blessings of being a Christian and how to live the Christian life.
- Don't forget the Old Testament or we'll start to comm-unicate that it is irrelevant.

---

1   Extract from *30 Stories for Taiwan's Working Class: A Prayer Guide*. OMF, 2006.

'Teenage' Christians

Do not assume that teenage Christians have a good overall Bible understanding. Some may have a grasp of all the basics whereas others may be familiar with some topics and unaware of others. Think carefully where the disciple needs to grow and be challenged. Consider the following options:

- A Bible overview.
- Increase informal discipleship time and teach skills in evangelism, discipleship and service. Reflect the practical skills in Bible study.
- A Gospel. Consider looking at specific teachings but don't do something that they've done numerous times and are already 'bored' with, unless you're an excellent discipler and want to prove that there is always so much more to learn even in the familiar.
- A selection of New and Old Testament books applicable to their situation.

More Mature Christians

This group need to be encouraged into service and discipleship of other Christians. We also need to help them grapple with more difficult questions. Consider the following options:

- Preparing Bible studies of their own, letting them read through the text until they can discern the overall theme, and then looking at how to divide the passage up and highlight main themes, and so on.
- Spending increasing amounts of time in evangelism and discipleship and strengthening their skills in these areas. Encourage them to do more on their own, but allow time for feedback and discussion.
- Formal weekly times may no longer be necessary but may be needed if a particular issue arises. Topical studies can be useful at this stage.
- Help the disciple set personal goals and monitor their own progress.

Deciding Which Gospel is the Most Suitable

Matthew

Written for a Jewish audience, it starts with a genealogy and often refers to the Old Testament. This may make it frustrating to someone with little Bible knowledge. It is the longest Gospel, but has some wonderful and challenging ethical teaching sections and some excellent parables that are exclusive to it.

Mark

The shortest and simplest Gospel, it is suitable for young people and those who find study hard. Two difficulties are that it doesn't start at the beginning of Jesus' life but when He is already 30, and that a portion at the end is identified as 'not in some early manuscripts'. You would need to be prepared for a more lengthy discussion on the reliability of the Bible.

Luke

This starts from before Jesus' birth and logically progresses through Jesus' life. It contains a mixture of teaching and miracles and is the basis of the Jesus film[2], so could be used alongside that for those who prefer visual learning.

John

This also does not start with Jesus' birth and is much more philosophical. It is most suitable for deep, reflective thinkers or people with a strong church background who need to be challenged a little.

As we gain in experience as disciplers, and learn more about people, our ability to choose suitable books of the Bible will improve.

---

2   The Jesus film is available online at www.jesusfilm.org in 90- and 120-minute versions. It is available in a wide range of languages and can be watched in one sitting or in shorter sections to accompany your Bible study.

Reflection:

For each of the disciples below choose a suitable Bible book to study.[3]

1. A person who has made a 'decision' at a meeting but has little grasp of sin or salvation. You're not even sure whether they are a Christian.
2. A new Christian who has many bad habits from their past life.
3. A new Christian who has never learnt how to relate to people.
4. A new believer who is being swayed by the legalistic teachings of a cult.
5. A Muslim-background believer who is familiar with the Quran but not the Bible.
6. A new church leader in a church that lacks leadership and a helpful structure.
7. A mature believer who has suffered tremendous personal loss.
8. A once missions-minded church has become very internally focused and you're discipling one of the church leaders.
9. A new believer who is not very clear about their own beliefs, and in danger of being deceived.
10. A family led to faith recently but non-committal about attending church.
11. Someone being persecuted and wanting to give up.
12. A Jewish-background believer with skewed or limited understanding of the Old Testament.
13. A Roman Catholic-background believer.

---

3 Answers can be found in Appendix C on p. 149.

11: How to Study the Bible

Topical Bible Study

A topical Bible study is taking a theme or topic and looking at it throughout the Bible. It involves taking verses from a variety of books and comparing them. It can be helpful in understanding the Bible's overall teaching on a particular issue.

What does a topical Bible study communicate to a new Christian?

First of all we are probably embarrassing the new believer with this approach, when they cannot find the books or verses. Put yourself in the place of a new Christian faced with a topical Bible study which flips all over the Bible. The whole process is humiliating.

Also we will waste time finding the verses and the disciple is likely to become confused about how the texts fit together and where they are in the Bible. Unconsciously we are also teaching the new believer that the Bible is more like an encyclopedia than normal literature where you start at the beginning and read to the end. Major ideas can be lost if books are not read as they were written. The disciple may also feel daunted that they'll never be able to find out where the topics are and may begin to depend on an 'expert' if they are to understand anything. We are also subconsciously underlining the message that 'not all the Bible is relevant'. It looks like only certain places and key verses are useful, and we can end up conveying what we think are the most important passages, rather than looking at all the verses and letting the disciple draw their own conclusions. The discipler is in danger of unconsciously skewing a topic, and the disciple is much more likely to be misled by false teaching if they haven't learnt to put things in context and draw their own conclusions by looking at all the verses.

Topical studies can also lead to a disciple feeling judged, if we especially choose subjects such as anger, that they may think we are applying directly to them. If a verse happens to come up in a book we are progressively studying, they can't so easily accuse us of choosing the study to point out their faults.

It is interesting to note though that lots of pre-prepared Bible study materials for new Christians do use a topical approach. Have a look through the resources in the shop before buying any to see what kind of passages they use. Remember to have a look at systematic materials too. Many of the New Testament books cover a lot of the same topics as the specific 'new Christian' resources, but will require less flicking through the Bible and will help the new believer learn to study the Bible for themselves.

Systematic Bible Study

A systematic Bible study works progressively through a single book, looking at the themes that arise in that book.

Some Benefits

1. It fits in with how the Bible was written. The Bible wasn't written with a topical, encyclopedia-like format. There is a purpose for that, and studying whole books quickly helps us to realize that each book was written for a purpose and has a central theme. The way the Bible was written is also far more natural for the non-Western mind to understand.

2. It allows us to grasp the whole message of each book. The logic and connections between each of the chapters and books of the Bible will become more visible.
3. It quickly gives the new Christian confidence that if they keep re-reading the passage, in its context, then the Holy Spirit will help them to understand the text. This will increase the disciple's confidence to independently read the Bible.
4. The disciple will become more dependent on God and less dependent on the discipler.
5. It suggests that all parts of the Bible are important and relevant, and models the appropriate way to interpret the Bible, book by book, chapter by chapter.
6. It forces the discipler to tackle passages that they might otherwise avoid. We are always tempted to avoid the tough bits.

SO THEN, IS THERE ANY PLACE FOR TOPICAL BIBLE STUDY?

Topical Bible study is not wrong, but we must be aware that it is far more difficult to do well and can be dangerous. It is much easier to manipulate the Bible to say what we want it to say if we are skipping about the Bible and taking single verses out of context.

An easier way to handle topical studies is to study a book and wait until the topics come up naturally. For example, you might be studying Matthew. During the course of that day's Bible study an issue like 'forgiveness' comes up. If this is a big issue in the person's life then you could explore the topic more fully, cross-referencing across the Bible and relating back to the original passage in Matthew. Or once you have completed a book, you could spend a few weeks looking at topics that came up in that book, before moving on to the next book. Thus, whole-book Bible study is the foundation, and topics come out of that.

I think one of the reasons that topical Bible study is so popular is that people don't know or aren't convinced that studying whole books of the Bible will cover what is necessary. Every book of the Bible is full of relevant topics that just come up naturally.

Reflection:

1. Choose one book of the Bible and go through it listing all the topics it contains.
2. Make a list of topics you think discipling would need to address and try to think in which books of the Bible those topics are covered. If you wanted to cover those topics, which books of the Bible might you start with to do so via the 'whole-book' Bible study method?

BIBLE STUDY MATERIALS

1. Not using any materials

This kind of discipleship simply involves choosing a book of the Bible and reading it through slowly, discussing any issues as they arise.

Benefits:
- Nil or minimum preparation time.
- Demonstrates that no fancy materials are needed to do discipleship.
- Can make the disciple feel that they and the discipler are just two people learning together.

Disadvantages:
- You'll probably grow less because you aren't forced to wrestle with the Bible as you prepare materials.
- It is very easy to just be lazy and not prepare at all and it will show. The disciple may feel you do not really care or value the study.
- You need to be good at asking questions and generating discussion.

2. Using materials prepared by others

This is a common way to start learning how to disciple. It is more relaxed and allows the new discipler to focus on things other than worrying about preparing Bible study materials.

Benefits:
- Allows you to pick and choose from a whole range of pre-prepared materials.
- You can choose materials that you've benefited from in the past.
- Removes some of the burden and anxiety you may feel at discipling another.

Disadvantages:
- You can become lazy and not prepare beforehand, and this will show.
- The materials are not tailor-made and might need adjusting. This is especially the case when using materials with those from other cultures. You need to be very discerning that the materials are helpful and are targeting issues in the individual's life.
- You need to be discerning that the materials are in fact teaching the Bible. Just because materials are published doesn't mean they are trustworthy and ones you want to use. Assess them in relation to what you want your disciple to learn and be influenced by. Remember that a disciple will usually follow the model they've been exposed to when they start to disciple someone else.
- Pre-prepared materials can be expensive.
- Again you miss out on the benefits of really grappling with the Bible yourself.

3. Preparing your own materials
This can be quite time-consuming but allows you to tailor a Bible study exactly to a disciple's needs.

Benefits:
- The Bible study is tailor-made to the individual. You can re-use the materials with different people and simply adjust as necessary.

- You will grow tremendously as a Christian yourself as you study the Bible in preparation.

Disadvantages:
- It can take a lot of time, especially as you may need to read some other books or commentaries to make sure you have understood the main points and messages of the passage.

This topic is a whole other book on its own,[1] but here are some basic steps for preparing your own material:

HERE ARE THE BASIC STEPS:

1. First pray, asking God to help you understand His Word and to be able to prepare the Bible study.

2. Read the whole book of the Bible you've chosen at least three times. You need to keep reading it until you begin to work out the main theme(s).

3. Do any background reading (from the Bible) that might be linked to your book. For example, many of Paul's letters have their background in Acts. Many of the prophets have the background to their times in Kings and Chronicles. Often the book will give you a clue by listing the kings who were reigning at the time of the prophet's ministry.

4. Ask the six basic questions – what, when, where, why, how and who?

5. Write one sentence that sums up the main theme of the book. Try to turn that sentence into a question that the whole book answers.

6. Slowly work out where the natural divisions come in the book. Please note that sometimes the chapter and verse divisions are very unhelpful. Also be careful of the highlighted headings that are in many Bibles. These are added by the publisher and are not part of God's Word. Most of the time they're helpful but I've seen some very misleading ones. Originally the Bible

---

1   *Leading Better Bible Studies*, K. Morris and R. Morris. Aquila Press, 1997.

didn't have chapter and verse divisions. They've been added for our benefit so we can find places more easily. Ignore them if necessary.

7. Sometimes you will find that the author returns to the same topic several times through the letter; you might want to group those sections together in one study. Try to work out how each section relates back to the main theme.

8. Write the questions for the Bible study. The questions should aim to help the disciple comprehend and apply the text. Write no more than six questions in total for the whole Bible study (two to three is even better). Avoid questions which have short answers as these will not encourage discussion.

12: DIFFERENT TYPES OF DISCIPLE

I have a friend who is the despair of every preacher as he always falls asleep in the sermon. You could conclude that he has a chronic sleep deprivation problem or just isn't interested in Jesus. Neither of these is true. My friend just finds it almost impossible to learn by sitting still and listening.

Most church activities cater best for visual and auditory learners – people who find it easy to learn by sitting and listening. Those less adept at this kind of study are often regarded as poor students, may fall asleep in sermons and fail to thrive in Bible studies. These individuals are left feeling stupid and are often neglected in churches.

People are different. This is so obvious that you would think it was a waste of time to say it. But when it comes to teaching in church we expect everyone to fit the same mould. People aren't just different in their personalities, but also in the way they learn.

Reflection:
1. Reflect back over your life. Can you remember a time when you had an excellent spiritual learning experience? What helped you to learn then?

2. What frustrating spiritual learning experiences have you had? Why?
3. Look at the chart below and work out what is your primary learning preference.

Visual/Auditory/Kinaesthetic Preferences[1]

	VISUAL	AUDITORY	KINAESTHETIC
When you spell, do you	Write it to see if it 'looks right'?	Use the 'sounding it out' approach?	Write it to find out if it 'feels right'?
When you concentrate, do you	Get distracted by untidiness?	Get distracted by noise?	Get distracted by movement?
When you are meeting people, do you	Forget names but remember faces?	Forget faces but remember names?	Remember best what you did together?
When you contact people, do you	Prefer a direct (face-to-face) personal meeting?	Prefer the telephone?	Talk while walking or another activity?
When you are relaxing, do you	Prefer to watch TV, read or see a play?	Prefer to listen to radio/CDs?	Prefer to play games or sport?
When you enjoy the arts, do you	Like painting?	Like music?	Like dancing?
When you try to interpret someone's mood, do you	Primarily look at facial expression?	Listen for the tone of the voice?	Watch body movements?
When you are reading, do you	Like descriptive scenes that you can visualize?	Enjoy dialogue, conversation and well-structured phrases?	Prefer action stories, or not a keen reader?

---

1 Adapted from *Leading Better Bible Studies*, K. Morris and R. Morris, Aquila Press, 1997, and *Honey and Mumford Learning Styles Questionnaire*, www.peterhoney. com, MTS Ltd, 2005

When you learn, do you	Like to see posters, diagrams, slides, demonstrations?	Like verbal instructions, talks and lectures?	Prefer direct involvement, activities and tasks?
Total	V:	A:	K:

Most people have a predominant learning style but this does not mean we are unable to learn in any other way. The best learning experiences combine all three sorts of learning. Anybody would get bored and disinterested if a study was exactly the same every week so using a variety of approaches is usually best.

Reflection:

Group the different learning methods below under the different learning styles (some may suit more than one learning style).[2]

* On-the-job evangelism
* Group discussion
* Research
* Feedback
* Reading
* E-learning (self-learning on the internet)
* Coaching/mentoring
* Observing
* Drawing and mapping
* Lectures
* Goal-setting
* Case studies
* Role-playing

---

2   Answers can be found in Appendix D on p. 153.

* Films and videos
* Questions and answers
* Drama
* Writing music or poetry in response to the Bible

How do we learn?

Adult education experts refer to the Learning Cycle[3], a summary of the four stages that an individual goes through when trying to learn new skills and information.

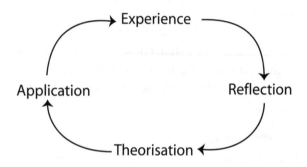

Although all stages are involved in learning, individuals will have preferences for different parts of the cycle. Some people love new experiences and getting out there and doing something. They are called **activists**. These disciples will generally love starting a new series of Bible study but their enthusiasm can slump if they haven't had a change in a while. They'll love anything creative and active. They'll really benefit from accompanying you to try out evangelism and other practical ministry skills. They'll have a tendency to rush on to the next experience and will need to be encouraged to reflect and think through their experiences.

---

3   Adapted from *Leading Better Bible Studies,* K. Morris and R. Morris. Aquila Press, 1997, and *Honey and Mumford Learning Styles Questionnaire,* www.peterhoney. com, MTS Ltd, 2005.

Others like to reflect on the experience. These **Reflectors** prefer plenty of time to think through the various aspects and to look at the experience from different perspectives. They need time to think and may often get left behind in Bible studies. Reflectors would benefit from being given reflection activities for homework, so they can come to the formal discussion time ready to share.

Theorists love seeing principles and gathering the facts together and coming up with a coherent theory. They may need help realizing that not everything can be fitted into a theory and will need encouraging to practically apply principles learned.

Pragmatists love to ask 'what difference will this make to my life?'; 'what's the point of this?' They often want to rush through the other stages of the learning cycle and 'get on with the important stuff.' They need to be helped to realize that what the Bible says in its own context is important and that rushing on to application can be unhelpful.

After 9/11 I had a number of disciples asking questions about the 'War on Terror' and whether this could be regarded as a 'Holy War'. They wanted me to quickly share my thoughts on this topic. However, to adequately answer this question it is important to understand what Holy War was in the Old Testament. I remember these activists getting frustrated at having to do so much background, but I insisted that they couldn't come up with correct application until they'd understood the Bible in its context and then applied it to today. After doing the hard work of understanding the Bible, they were surprised that they came up with quite different answers to their own questions than what they'd previously felt to be correct.

In summary,

ACTIVISTS	REFLECTORS
* Like new experiences and are quickly bored * Like concrete experiences * Think quickly * Like short sessions and plenty of variety * Like to participate and have fun * Like to experiment * Willing to take risks and try something without much preparation * Like to initiate * Easily bored by traditional Bible study and by series over 6 weeks long	* Like making observations and reflecting * Like trying to work out cause/effect, see patterns * Like analysis and trying to understand before putting into action * Like thorough preparation * Can get left behind on the topic and then frustrate others by returning to earlier topic later * Like to make decisions at their own speed * Often the quiet ones in a Bible study and better listeners because they view people's experience as valuable
PRAGMATISTS	THEORISTS
* Like the application stage of learning best * Like testing implications or concepts in new situations * Like activities to be real and practical * Prepared to try out new ideas early and 'tailor-make' them to their context * More businesslike in meetings and discussions * More focused on objectives and goals * Want to see relevance! * Become frustrated if no outcome is reached	* Love to see the overall picture * Formation of abstract concepts and generalisations, rules and principles which help explain experience * Like to feel intellectually stretched * Like structure and clear objectives * Like logical presentation of ideas * More disciplined and tidier * More tolerant of models and theories and explaining their relevance * Can get bogged down in minute details

Don't get hung up with analysing your disciple's preferred learning style though. Unless they have a strong preference, most people will learn in a variety of settings. But understanding what is happening in our discipling sessions will help us to be more tolerant of our differences and allow us to think through how to encourage our disciple on, so that the whole cycle is worked through.

It is important that we understand how we, and the person we are discipling, prefer to learn, so we can better disciple the individual and challenge them to work on those areas they find hardest. God never forgets that we are individuals, but we all need to learn how to spend quiet time with God, to reflect on the Word, to put God's Word into practice and to communicate the gospel in innovative ways.

Reflection:

1. Look at Matthew 8:23-9:8. How could you teach this to disciples with the three different learning styles?
2. Think of a skill (e.g. learning to pray, doing your own daily Bible reading, sharing your testimony). How could you teach this, combining a number of different learning styles?
3. Think of a friend and try to classify their current stage in the learning cycle. What would you do to engage them in the best way?

13: Dealing with Tough Issues

In every discipling relationship there will be times when we will need to talk about something we find difficult. Most of us find it difficult to discuss personal topics such as sin related to ethics or sexual issues. The temptation is to avoid the issues and hope that they go away. But to fail to address them means that both of us stunt our growth.

As a 17-year-old, my roommates took me aside and talked to me about my pessimism and how it was destroying my relationships. Perhaps they weren't as sensitive as they could have been, but I cried because I knew what they said was true. Often our first reaction to being confronted is tears or anger. That is one of the reasons why people don't like to confront others. Soon after my friends confronted me, I went to them and thanked them. Their courage led to big changes in my life and I now look back and evaluate friends by their willingness to confront me. Those with that kind of courage I rate very highly, for they truly love me.

Reflection:
1. What issues do you find difficult to confront? Why?
2. Can you think of a time when someone confronted you inappropriately? How did you feel?

3. What about a more positive experience? What was the outcome of these experiences?

Some Principles

Matthew 18:15-17 gives us some helpful pointers in dealing with tough issues:

> 'If your brother sins against you, go and show him his fault, just between the two of you. If he listens to you, you have won your brother over. But if he will not listen, take one or two others along, so that "every matter may be established by the testimony of two or three witnesses." If he refuses to listen to them, tell it to the church; and if he refuses to listen even to the church, treat him as you would a pagan or a tax collector.'

1. Approach someone personally in a one-to-one situation. Never humiliate a person in public. It is also important not to first discuss the situation with someone else. First, go and try to solve the problem just between the two of you. We have a bad habit of gossiping with others first.

2. If the person won't listen and refuses to face the issue or repent as appropriate, then we are to take one or two others along to confront them.

3. Only if steps one or two have failed is something to become general knowledge and be dealt with in public. If this still has no impact, then v. 17 says that they should be asked to leave the church. The whole purpose of this radical step is so that they can see the enormity of the problem and repent. It is designed for the good of the person and the church. This is aimed at someone who refuses to even recognise their sin and repent, not at someone whose attitude is right but they continue to fail. The purpose of stages one and two is to ensure that stage three isn't reached at all. That is, the idea is to deal with issues while they are still small and before they become major issues.

Most issues that need to be dealt with are raised naturally in the course of Bible study. This is one of the miracles of systematic Bible study. We may not even be aware of the issue and suddenly the disciple will be saying, 'I've been wrong in this area and need to do something about it.' Studying the Bible this way lets God raise the correct issues in His time. Systematic study also means that when an issue comes up the disciple is less able to say, 'You did this to accuse me.' You could be less direct by using questions to help the disciple think through an issue for himself or by using a story as the prophet Nathan did with David.

What about an obvious issue that needs addressing straight away?
Principle 1: Pray, Pray, Pray
Pray that God prepares the disciple's heart and keeps our motives pure, only ever confronting for the good of the other person. Pray for wisdom and gentleness as we speak and that God will convict the disciple of their sin.

Principle 2: The Only Authority is the Bible
That is, we don't raise issues because we are bothered by something and want to make the person into our image. We only raise issues that the Bible lets us know are important. We refer to the Bible's teaching on the issue, not using any authority we think we might have.

Principle 3: Speak the Truth in Love
The disciple needs to know that we only address the issue because we want them to grow more and more like Jesus. Speaking lovingly is helped if we keep our voice gentle. It is perhaps wise to address the issue rather indirectly at first and only get more direct if they fail to acknowledge or address their issue. One of the best ways to address an issue may be to share a testimony of how God helped us to deal with the same issue. Being real and sharing our own failures is very encouraging. If we always appear to be perfect, then the disciple won't accept criticism so easily. Sometimes we can just share about our struggles with an issue

we know the disciple is struggling with too. They may naturally say, 'I struggle with that too', opening up a conversation easily.

Principle 4: Don't be Afraid or Embarrassed by Emotion
Being confronted by our sin is hard to cope with. The end result will hopefully be repentance and growth but this can be a hard task and we should expect emotion. Be ready to help the disciple through the difficulties.

Principle 5: Plan a Confrontation if Possible
Think and pray before you raise an issue. Don't confront someone before you are sure it is the right thing to do and you have thought about how to help the disciple once you have pointed out their sin. Think also about what is best for the disciple. For example, don't try to deal with issues the night before their exams start.

Principle 6: Listen
It is so easy to have our own plans and just to rush on. We need to learn to really listen and not try to guess other people's thoughts or assume we know all about the issues. We might discover that there is a much deeper issue. For example, someone might have low self-esteem but we may discover that they were sexually abused as a child. That will take much longer and need much more sensitivity to deal with than the original issue.

Principle 7: Work With Them on a Solution
If we simply tell someone they are doing something wrong, we haven't helped them at all. We need to discuss the issue with them and then work with them on trying to solve it. Telling them an answer does not encourage them to depend on God, or listen to what He has to say to them. Spend time really thinking about what the Bible has to say on an issue.

Principle 8: Dealing with Denial
If a person isn't willing to admit or address an issue, then close the session and ask them to go away and think about it. Usually

they will come back later when they are ready to discuss how they might change. There might be a rare situation where you'd need to say that continuing to disciple this person is impossible unless they repent and deal with the issue confronting them. Be sensitive, though; not everyone will want to talk about a problem, though they may be dealing with it privately. Give the disciple time to see if this is the case before taking further action.

Principle 9: Always End With Prayer
Praying with someone is a great way to finish. Make sure that your prayer really reminds them of who God is and talks of the hope and forgiveness that He provides.

Using the Sword of the Spirit
In Ephesians 6:10ff, Paul tells us that every Christian is involved in a spiritual battle. How many of us really believe that Satan hates us and likes nothing better than seeing us wallowing in despair, fear and worry, and trapped by sin?

However, as Christians, God has graciously given us everything we need to resist sin and the devil. Jesus has already defeated him when He rose from the dead; we just need to implement this defeat in our lives.

You might ask, well, why is Satan still so powerful and active if he's already been defeated? Good question. It is rather like what happens when you spray a cockroach with insecticide. When the spray touches it, the cockroach doesn't die instantly, but for a few minutes seems even more alive than previously. It runs around furiously but suddenly falls on its back, wriggles its legs and then dies. Once the spray has touched the cockroach, its end is certain. Although for a short time it might appear even more energetic, it will inevitably die. Satan is somewhat like that. Jesus' resurrection guaranteed that his end is certain. Meanwhile, he seems even more energetic in his desire to destroy God's people. But if we stand on God's promises we need not be drawn in by Satan's lies. If we trust in Jesus, Satan cannot harm us no matter how much he tries.

Ephesians 6 tells us that God has given us weapons against Satan. There are five defensive weapons: the helmet of salvation, the breastplate of righteousness, the shield of faith, the belt of truth and the shoes of the readiness of the gospel. But there is also one offensive weapon: 'the sword of the Spirit which is the Word of God.' That is, God's promises in the Bible are our offensive against the devil. By claiming the truths that God has already told us, we can overcome Satan's lies and start understanding the truth: Jesus' victory. Though this weapon is available to us all, most of us leave it rusting from disuse.

Here's an example of how to use the Sword of the Spirit to overcome tough issues and temptations:

Susan was a keen Christian who really wanted to serve the Lord. But her low self-esteem and fear of failure, incompetence and rejection severely affected her ability to minister to others and try new things. So I explained to her how to practically use her 'sword'…

'I want you to write down various Bible passages that refer to the issue of fear.'

Susan wrote down a long list including these verses: John 10:28, Romans 8:31, 1 Corinthians 1:27-29 and Hebrews 13:5 which pointed out that God was all-powerful, would never forsake us, delighted in using weak people and could not be overcome by Satan.

I suggested to Susan that she either memorize or go through the general ideas of these verses first thing in the morning and last thing before bed. Also, every time she had fearful thoughts she was immediately to remind herself of these verses, learning to 'take every thought captive' (2 Cor. 10:5 ESV). Susan actually chose her own method, which was to pick one verse at a time to memorize and have that as her verse for the week.

The results came faster than either of us expected. On the second morning of her new 'sword fighting' regime, Susan suddenly sat up in bed and said, 'I'm not scared. For the first morning of my life, I'm not scared to face the day!' Exciting as this was, it is not the signal to put down the sword and let it rust again. It is merely a signal that God is proving His promises, and that 'sword fighting' is God's way.

Susan continues to deal with issues in this way. Sometimes she doesn't fight and so slides into a period of bondage to Satan's lies, but when she starts believing God's promises again, she quickly experiences victory. Susan is radically changed from the woman of a year ago. Now, she is no longer controlled by her emotions, but is free to serve and glorify God. She is currently applying to do Christian work overseas, which is something she wouldn't have dared to do a year ago.

Case Studies:
How would you confront these issues?[115]

1.   Mark is a successful businessman who became a Christian two years ago and has grown steadily. But he still mistreats his employees. He pays them poorly and often scolds them. Unsurprisingly, he has not led any of them to faith.

2.   Rachel is one of the top teachers in the local high school. She came to faith six months ago and has noticed that most members of the church do not study the Bible as seriously as she does. She complains to you about their lack of commitment.

3.   Deborah has been a faithful church member for several years. However, she does not have a spiritual gift that brings her much attention. You have just discovered that she sometimes spreads gossip about leaders whom she envies.

4.   Sarah is the mother of five children. Her husband is a casual labourer whose employment is spasmodic. Sarah cannot always meet the basic needs of their children, so she frequently buys a lottery ticket in the hopes of winning a large sum of money that will help them out.

5.   Jack is a high-school student. He is often tempted to visit websites with sexually explicit material. He has just admitted to you that he now daydreams often about having sex with his girlfriend.

---

1   Answers can be found in Appendix E on p. 155.

PART THREE:

PASSING ON
USEFUL SKILLS

14: Discipleship
That Transfers Skills

The Book of Acts lists Paul as having travelled and worked with Barnabas, John Mark (Acts 13ff), Silas, Timothy (Acts 16ff) and Luke (Acts 20:7ff) as well as others such as Sopater from Berea, Aristarchus and Secundas from Thessalonica, Gauis from Derbe, and Tychicus and Trophimus from the province of Asia (Acts 20:4). Many of these were brand-new Christians and Paul took them along with him to the churches of Macedonia and Greece, where they would have been watching and then increasingly been involved in ministering to the new churches in the area. In Troas they saw someone raised from the dead and were part of the all-night teaching event (Acts 20:7-12). Presumably they also heard Paul's farewell to the Ephesian elders (Acts 20:13-38) and heard how he trained and ministered to church leaders, before perhaps going on to Jerusalem and learning of the persecution that comes as part of being a Christian.

Jesus too modelled many aspects of ministry such as prayer, healing, preaching, teaching, evangelism, dealing with conflict and suffering. He sent His disciples out on 'practice' ministry trips (Luke 9, 10), giving them specific instructions including what to wear and how they were to find accommodation, warning them they may not be welcome. We don't know if these ministry trips happened only twice or more often, or how long they were out ministering. But we can see that Jesus first modelled the ministries before sending out the twelve to Jewish villages. When the disciples returned, Jesus took time to debrief them - listening to their experiences and no doubt offering advice, but also warning them not to get carried away by the spectacular but to keep their eyes focused on the gospel.

Jesus didn't just aim to change the disciples' beliefs, attitudes and behaviour but also to teach them the new skills they would need to grow the church. Jesus taught the disciples how to preach, cast out demons, deal with opposition and pray. And He taught all these skills by first modelling them to the disciples and then giving them time to practise those skills.

As Jesus first modelled the skills and then gave the disciples opportunities to practise, so it is best to follow this kind of model. Jesus was preparing the disciples for the time when He would leave them and return to heaven. At that point they needed to learn to rely on the wisdom and resources of the Holy Spirit. We also should be encouraging our disciple to rely on God and not on us doing all the work for them. There is a helpful acronym that can assist us: MAWL.

M–Model
Run through a certain skill with the disciple, showing them how to do it, and then let them go away and have a try.

For example, after some time of being discipled themselves we may suggest they find someone to disciple. They've experienced being discipled. After teaching them some of the principles of how to get started we'll pray together for an appropriate person.

A–Assist
Once the disciple has tried it out, we need to give them the opportunity of feedback. We may need to go over the task again, giving further hints and tips, or work through an example with them.

In the learning-to-disciple example, we may make suggestions for the first few sessions and let them try them out and come back to discuss what happened.

W–Watch

Continue following up with the disciple on how the skill is developing. Give further assistance if necessary but give them the opportunity to try things out and learn by themselves.

Some weeks into the new discipling experience we might accompany our disciple and watch how they go; afterwards, we can give appropriate feedback.

L–Leave

Assistance will become less and less necessary and eventually the disciple will be able to use the skill completely unaided. At times we may need to help them think through some of the more complex issues but essentially they will be able to get on without our help.

Eventually the disciple is discipling someone else without any assistance from us.

The length of time from 'Modelling' to 'Leaving' will be different for each skill. Something like evangelism is an area needing multiple skills and can take far longer to learn and become proficient at than having a regular personal Bible study, for example. The main thing is to check that you are encouraging the disciple towards independence from us and onto dependence on the Holy Spirit.

Skills training is something that can happen alongside Bible study. It doesn't need to be a separate session. For example, teaching conflict resolution works well when there is some conflict that needs to be resolved. The disciple will be much more open to learning at that time.

Some skills are more appropriate to teach early on and others are for more mature believers, so think through which skills are most important for your disciple to learn.

Reflection:

Look at the 20 skills listed here. Try to rearrange them into an order so that easier skills are at the beginning of the list and the list ends with harder skills that you might want to develop for a more mature Christian going into leadership.

- Personal Bible reading/study
- Conflict resolution
- Prayer
- Using a gospel outline
- Meeting with other believers
- Leading a meeting
- Answering tough questions that non-Christians ask
- Diagnosing where people are at spiritually
- Leading a Bible study
- Confession of sin
- Preaching
- Stewardship of money
- Guidance of the Holy Spirit and discernment
- Praying for others
- Scripture memorization
- Fighting temptation
- Using spiritual gifts
- Sharing own testimony
- Leading non-preaching part of church service
- Discipling others

Which skills might you add? Which do you think your disciple is already competent in?

15: Teaching Someone to Pray

You are meeting up with someone for a time of formal discipleship each week, and every session you discuss the Bible and share with each other. You so enjoy talking that often prayer is squeezed into the last few minutes and sometimes skipped altogether. You often talk during the week or phone but you never pray in any of these more casual times. When the disciple has problems you always rush in with solutions.

What will this disciple have learnt about prayer?

The way we pray reveals our beliefs about prayer. Unfortunately our model will pass on to our disciple. Would we be happy for our disciples to have our prayer lives? Prayer suffers from being much talked about in theory, but often neglected in practice. I'm sure you would say that you believe that prayer is important. Such words as 'first priority' and 'essential' might spring to mind. However, would others looking at our lives from the outside be able to draw that conclusion about our beliefs? If we always relegate prayer to the last minute, then we model that prayer is unimportant and irrelevant. In the same way, if we pray as though it is a boring duty, what do we say about our belief in prayer? So many of us have fine thoughts about prayer, but do we actually pray?

Prayer is a constant struggle and we shouldn't be surprised at this. Someone has wisely said, 'Satan laughs at our toiling, mocks at our wisdom, but trembles when we pray.'[116] Satan knows that a prayerless life will be a powerless life. So he will direct a lot of time to making sure we are distracted from prayer. How often have I had thoughts suggesting that really I should be out sharing the gospel or writing a letter to encourage someone rather than praying. God would never tempt me to substitute activity for prayer. I have often wondered how some Christian leaders and missionaries achieved so much. How could they possibly have fitted in what they had to do? What was their secret? James Hudson Taylor (founder of the China Inland Mission, now OMF International) would spend hours in prayer. That was his spiritual secret. More time in prayer actually helped him set priorities and made him far more efficient with the time he had.

Reflection:
1. Set some prayer goals for your personal prayer times.

So let's go back to the basics we want to model and pass on to our disciples.

Why Pray?
It is important to explain why we are praying in the first place. This is especially true in cross-cultural situations where a person may be used to a non-Christian form of prayer. In Chinese religions, for example, prayer is nearly always related to manipulating the gods to get what you want. There is no aspect of real relationship there. Thanksgiving and true praise are rare, if not unheard of. There may be a formula to chant, and it is not necessarily something done on a regular basis but rather when you need something. It is aimed at being fervent and done correctly to convince the gods to answer your requests. If one god fails, you move on to another. You can see that there

---

1   Anonymous.

are a lot of potential misconceptions in this situation that need to be dealt with.

So, do we pray because God needs our prayer? Does He get lonely without us? No! Part of the mystery of the Trinity is that God is always in perfect, fulfilled relationship within Himself: Father, Son and Spirit. Though He knows what we need before we ask for it (Matt. 6:8), He still delights for us to communicate with Him and loves to hear our questions and thoughts and have us ask Him for the things we need.

However, it seems to me that the person who benefits most from prayer is yourself. Prayer helps us to increasingly see the world how God sees it. The more we practise praise and thankfulness, the more we will experience the great joy that comes from trusting God. Prayer also helps us to express our love to God and teaches us to depend on Him for everything. So often our prayerlessness reflects the fact that there are areas that we now think we are competent in and no longer need God's help. We only pray when things get out of control. If people treated us like that, we'd say they were manipulating us and the relationship wouldn't last long.

It is important to remember that Satan is real and hates to see Christians mature in Christ. Mature Christians are dangerous to him and his purposes, so he'll use every means to oppose us. Two areas that will clearly come under attack are our prayer life and Bible study. Satan uses many methods like lies, doubt, deception and discouragement (Gen. 3, John 8:44, 2 Cor. 11:14, 1 Pet. 5:8). The question I often ask myself if I need to discern whether something is from Satan is, where will this action lead me? God will never encourage us to do something that will lead us away from Himself. Even something that is outwardly good can be used by Satan. For example, I love singing and would love to be in a choir. But if the result of being in the choir is that a great deal of my energy is diverted away from personal Bible study and prayer, and away from Christian service, then it is not right for me to do it (although it might be right for someone else). We need to constantly be seeking God's will and learning from Him. What Satan fears is the believers who cling to God and who constantly refresh themselves with the Living Water.

How should I Pray?

How to start and end prayers can be daunting, as can 'fancy' prayer language or a special prayer voice that is different to how the person speaks normally. God requires none of these things in our prayers, nor does He require any special posture or location. We can pray any time, anywhere, anyhow.

Encourage your disciple to use simple prayers, like normal speech, without Christian jargon, explaining that prayer doesn't have to be complicated. Everyday language will prevent people feeling they aren't 'good' enough to pray.

Suggest that they choose a start and ending that they feel comfortable with and make sure you explain the word 'Amen'. Most prayers end with this but it is a Hebrew word that someone is unlikely to understand unless it is explained. It simply means 'let it be so'[217] and is the traditional way that prayers were ended. Using this word is a widely understood signal that our prayer has ended, so that others know when we are finished. It is probably easiest to continue this tradition as it is used in the Bible and throughout the Christian world.

Remember to explain that prayer must be done in the disciple's own time as well as at formal prayer meetings. Remind them that God reads thoughts and so they don't need to pray out loud if they don't want to.

What Should I Pray For?

Prayer can be used to repent of our sin, to thank God and to ask Him for things for ourselves and others. Most people don't need to be reminded to ask God for things but may need help in doing the other things. A helpful acronym is ACTS:

---

2   *New Bible Dictionary (2nd Edition)*. Inter-Varsity Press, 1982.

A – Adoration
    Praise God for who He is
C – Confession
    Remember to admit your sin and ask forgiveness
T – Thanksgiving
    Praise God for the things He has done
S – Supplication
    Ask God for things for yourself and for others.

Start teaching your disciple by using single-sentence prayers thanking God for something from the Bible passage you've just studied, or for something good that has happened that week, and slowly progress to longer prayers incorporating all the different aspects.

Keeping a Prayer Diary

This idea is a simple way to teach people to make more specific requests so that they change from such requests such as 'bless my friend' to more specific requests such as 'help my friend to be able to share the gospel with her neighbour this week'. This diary helps our faith to grow as we see God answering our requests. It will also force us to consider why some requests are answered by a 'No' or a 'Wait'. The prayer diary idea allows us to follow up former requests and will help us in remembering to thank God. Perhaps use the following format:

Date Started Praying	Request	Date Answered and Yes/No
5th May	Find a prayer partner	17th May, Yes

Although I have a general pattern of prayer, praying at the beginning and end of a session, it is never an inflexible rule. Creativity and flexibility are important. Some weeks you might choose to pray for the entire time. It would be a great idea to pray together for an hour or two and model how to do that in an interesting way. As the disciple sees the discipler's enthusiasm, they will catch it.

Holding prayer meetings

After finishing Bible College, I worked in a Chinese church for a year. One Sunday, the church announced they were going to hold a half night of prayer the following week. Most of the congregation were probably too polite to say anything, but I think the general opinion was 'How boring that will be!'

The next Friday night, we started with a meal. After the main part of the meal, we looked at a Psalm and used that to start us off on a time of thanksgiving and praise to God. Throughout the night we changed styles and topic of prayer about every 30 minutes. At some time we also had a break for dessert. All of them were surprised when 11 p.m. arrived. They made comments like 'I never thought praying could be fun', 'I never thought we could pray for all that time', 'Let's do this again.'

Somehow we have associated prayer with boredom. Sadly, Christians and churches only have themselves to blame for this. Some of my most frustrating church meetings have been prayer meetings, where I have been bored because they are so unimaginative. Prayer times don't have to be like that. I want to demonstrate to all those I disciple that not only is prayer important and effective, but that it can be great fun.

Here are some ideas:

1. People are easily bored and easily tired. Try changing pace or content to keep people interested, or scheduling in refreshment breaks. Sometimes the break we need is simply to change our posture or style of praying.

2. If people are inspired they will want to be involved. Try to encourage people to see the purpose and impact of praying.

3. Variety keeps people awake, so try breaking the prayer into 15-30 minute sections. It can include praise, thanks, confession and prayer for a variety of topics, such as family, self, missionaries, church, non-Christian friends and upcoming evangelistic

opportunities. Use different media to give information for prayer, not just endless lists of prayer points.

4. Keep prayer balanced and God-focused. Perhaps start with reading a Bible passage and praising God as a reflection of what is read.

5. Be creative. God made us to be creative and so we should use our creativity.

6. Join with other people. Sometimes pray in pairs, sometimes alone and sometimes in threes or everyone in the group together. Change who you pray with; don't always pray with the same person. Have a time of quiet confession on your own.

7. Change your posture – sitting, standing, kneeling … walk around the neighbourhood and pray for it as God inspires you.

8. Use music as an inspiration to praise or as a response to God. People could choose one song that they'd like to sing to God.

9. Have prayer points printed out on a small card and pray for five minutes for that and then switch cards/ groups.

10. Use the newspaper to pray for current issues and situations facing the world or your local area. Perhaps use a map and pray for the local area and outreach in that area.

11. Share personal needs and put the person in the centre of the group and lay hands on them as you pray. This is very moving for all involved.

Reflection:

1. What have you found helpful in your personal prayer life? How could you share this?

2. What do you think it is good to pray about at the beginning of a session? Why?

3. If you were to have a two-hour prayer time with your disciple, how would you do it? How could you make it interesting so that they learn to love praying?

16: Teaching Someone To Do Personal Bible Study

Eva had been a Christian for 15 years. I started discipling her because I couldn't see much evidence of growth in her life and was concerned for her. She was pretty nervous about the whole idea of discipleship. As we chatted, I asked about her personal Bible study and prayer habits, referring to them as her 'quiet-time'. I have never forgotten her answer: 'What is a quiet-time? The pastor is always telling us to have one but I've never dared to ask him what he meant.'

To have a 'quiet-time', or do personal Bible study, is one of the very first things we should teach a disciple. Even some long-term Christians have never learnt the discipline of regularly reading the Bible themselves, or if they know it is important, still have little idea how to go about doing it.

The key to helping people begin having a quiet-time is to give them the confidence that they can understand the Bible and rely on the Holy Spirit to help them. Suggest some of the simpler or shorter books for them to begin with: a book based on stories, such as Mark, could be an easier introduction to Bible reading.

Reflection:

1. If they are not keen on reading, how could you help encourage them and give them confidence in reading the Bible?

How about using Bible tapes where the Bible is read, or even try preparing your own?

MODELLING A QUIET TIME

Pray

Begin with a prayer asking God to help you understand. It could be as simple as 'Dear Heavenly Father, thank you for your Word, the Bible. Please help us to understand it and apply it to our lives. Amen.'

Read

Choose a passage of suitable length. Don't try to cover a whole chapter to start with. A couple of verses could be enough. Suggest reading the passage twice.

Think and apply

Use a notebook to answer a few simple questions. For example:

- What does this passage teach about God?
- What do we learn about people in the passage?
- Are there things you don't understand? Can you find the answers in the passage? Suggest they write down questions so they can follow them up next time you meet.
- What is the main point of the passage?
- Is there a command to obey or an example to follow?

The aim is to give the disciple confidence that they can understand the Bible themselves, so don't give them the answers. Use questions to encourage their thoughts.

Pray

Encourage them to thank God for something they have learnt in the passage and to pray about how to apply it.

For someone learning to do personal Bible study, you should use this simple format for at least two weeks. They could continue on their own during the week, and then you meet to do the next section and discuss any questions and difficulties they've had.

WHEN AND WHERE?

Make sure you discuss with your disciple the practicalities of doing personal Bible study. Ask when they think it would be best to do their personal Bible study and how often they think they should do it. Don't jump in with your ideas straight away but let the disciple come up with something that suits them. When I asked a new Christian I am currently discipling what she thought about doing personal Bible study, she told me she had been reading her Bible twice a day, studying two different books simultaneously – one in the morning and one in the evening. If I'd just jumped in with my methods of personal Bible study without taking time to find out what she felt was suitable, I would have halved her Bible study time and stopped her creative way of looking at the Bible! There are lots of creative ways of doing personal Bible study, so work with your disciple to come up with some interesting ideas and encourage them to try out new ways of doing things.

====

Reflection:

1. Why do we struggle with doing personal Bible study?
2. What is the normal response and why?
3. What is the best way to deal with it?

As usual, Satan is out to keep us as far away from God as possible. Everyone struggles with personal Bible reading at some point, so encourage your disciple to keep going even when they do not feel like it. Nagging someone and making them feel a failure will never help. Sharing our own experiences and methods we have used to overcome the difficulties is a good way to encourage.

====

Reflection:

1. How did you learn to do personal Bible study? What was helpful to you?
2. Think of some alternative ideas for how to combine personal Bible reading with formal discipleship.

17: TRAINING
EVANGELISM SKILLS

For the majority of people, telling them something about evangelism will seldom lead to them going out and doing it.

I once spent four hours teaching a group of Australians how to do evangelistic Bible studies with non-Christians. I talked about the method and made them run through the method with each other. When two Mainland Chinese ladies arrived at the church, knowing nothing about Christianity but keen to find out, I thought it was the perfect opportunity for one of my students, who was fluent in Chinese, to try out her newly learnt skills. When I asked my Christian friend, though, she replied, 'Oh, I couldn't!' Her problem was fear, not inability.

A 'how to' manual on evangelism could fill several books, and still may not actually encourage a disciple to put their skills into practice. So I will leave the 'how to' to the books already written on the subject and focus on the principles for encouraging a disciple to actually set about sharing the gospel.

Principle 1: Opportunities
Pass keenly seeking non-Christians who would like to spend some time chatting things through on to your disciple, giving them a ready-made opportunity.

119

Principle 2: Prepare a Testimony

'Giving a testimony' is simply retelling what God has done for us. It needn't be complicated and it is good for us to be prepared to explain what being a Christian has meant for us.

A simple way to begin thinking about your testimony is using the before-and-after model. Perhaps choose one issue and describe what it was like before you became a Christian and what it is like after. This could start off as just a few sentences, for example:

> 'Before I knew Jesus, I tried to rely on myself. I always ended up exhausted and in despair. Now I've met Jesus, I pray and ask for His help and wisdom. I've been amazed at the difference it makes.'

As you get more confident you can think through other issues and expand on these. How you came to know Jesus is what most people think of when you say 'testimony', but other issues such as forgiveness, prayer, love, trust, coping with tough times, misunderstandings you had about the Bible, low self-esteem, anger or pride could make powerful stories about God's work in your life. These topics can be particularly powerful for those of us with what we consider 'boring testimonies'; for example, if we grew up in a Christian family and never had a distinct conversion experience. Remember, even 'boring' testimonies are important in helping other people realize that being 'good' isn't enough, that you aren't a Christian by default and that everyone needs to make a personal decision for Christ.

A basic format for a testimony, whatever the topic, could be as follows:

a. *CONNECT*: It is important to make our testimony relevant to those listening. Giving a few sentences about your background in a way that connects with the audience, will get their attention and make your testimony relevant. For example, mentioning your interest in sport to sport-crazy young people gives you common ground on which to relate.

b. *BEFORE*: Simply say what your life was like in terms of that issue before. Use emotion and speak in real terms. Explain how it affected your life and why it wasn't positive. Obviously we don't want people to go away thinking our past way of doing things was acceptable, so make sure you show why you needed Jesus' help even if you didn't know it at the time.

c. *JESUS*: Describe how knowing Jesus changed things. Perhaps a Bible verse or sermon really impacted on you?

d. *AFTER*: Compare how your life is different now. Don't use glib phrases but be honest about how much you have changed or what you still struggle with. Let people know that you're still not perfect and are a 'work in progress', but explain the benefits of living this new way and how Jesus is helping you.

e. *CHALLENGE*: Explain that Jesus can make a difference in your listeners' lives too. Give people a way of responding to what you have said. Suggest they can come and talk to you afterwards for the longer version, or perhaps point out people who can explain more about the gospel to them if they want to hear. Remember not to embarrass or condemn people though; this will seldom attract people to Jesus.

Let the disciple have a go preparing their testimony, then listen to it and give feedback. Try to arrange somewhere where they can actually share their testimony in public or with some acquaintances, even if it is just with Christian friends to start with.

Principle 3: Alternate Teaching and Practice
When teaching how to give a testimony or speak to non-Christians, first explain the principles, and then let your disciple see you in action. Share your testimony with your disciple, for example, then spend time evaluating what you said and how it could have been improved. Then let your disciple have a go, returning for debriefing after each experience.

Principle 4: Start Easy
Practising together first and gaining confidence is important. Beginning in a difficult situation is likely to put your new evangelist off completely. Perhaps practise with a 'safe' person, such as another Christian, to begin with, and then slowly move

121

on to tougher situations – sharing with a non-Christian family member or friend, for example. Saying 'I've just learnt how to share the main points of the Bible/my personal story and I wondered if you'd listen and let me know how to improve' could be a good way to begin sharing with non-Christians, and many are happy to help out. Pray with your disciples about finding suitable people to share with.

Principle 5: Don't Wait Until You're an Expert

You do not have to wait to teach others about evangelism until you are competent yourself. There is nothing wrong with learning together. You could both attend a training course or read one of the many excellent 'how to' books available[1]. Discuss each chapter and pray together for opportunities. Debrief and encourage each other on as you go.

Principle 6: Practise What You Preach

If the discipler often prays for non-Christians and tells of opportunities they've had to share the gospel, the disciple will soon catch their enthusiasm. If you are involved in outreach events, why not let your disciple accompany you as you talk to non-Christians and then talk about the situation afterwards.

Principle 7: Be Flexible

Methods for training evangelism skills will need to be different for every disciple. The time when you start training will vary immensely. Often it happens naturally when the disciple says, 'I was talking to someone this week and they asked this question ….' That is a good signal that the person is keen to learn. Conversely, if the disciple shows no interest in sharing their faith, it might be good to ask them why and then deal with the issues that are raised.

Principle 8: Ongoing Training

Even after 10 years doing evangelism and training others to do it, I'm still learning. You cannot expect to teach your disciple

---

1   *Know and Tell the Gospel*. John Chapman. Hodder and Stoughton, 1981 and *Just Walk Across the Room*, Bill Hybels. Zondervan, 2006.

everything, but keep trying to develop their skills until they are confident to speak to others and in the habit of doing so, and are able to evaluate experiences and see how to improve.

TRAINING TRAINERS
Are we aiming for addition or multiplication?

If we want the gospel to spread, we need to be multipliers. It may seem more impressive to be preaching to crowds and leading seminars, and those activities will no doubt receive more praise, but one person can only speak to a limited number of people. Even in discipling, most people will only be able to meet one or two others each year. But if we train those we are discipling also to disciple others then we will be vastly increasing the number of people hearing the gospel and growing in maturity.

Do the mathematics. One person reaching 100 a year for 20 years, or one person reaching one other person who in the following year also reaches and trains one who reproduces, and so on for 20 years. Which method will reach the most people?

How can we be multipliers?

From the very first week make it clear the disciple should be aiming to disciple someone else.

As early as possible find them someone to disciple, or give them opportunities to share with other people, Christians and non-Christians. Spend some of your discipleship time debriefing them on their own discipleship experiences. Begin praying together for a suitable person for the disciple to disciple. This will help them keep their eyes open for opportunities.

The Art of Debriefing
Debriefing simply means talking over what happened, evaluating, reflecting on and discussing the issues that arose. The role of the discipler is to ask questions that prompt the disciple to think through their experience. Possible questions could be:

- What do you think went well today?
- What did you find difficult?

- What did you notice about the person's response?
- How could you improve this session?

You could also practise answering questions the disciple struggled with or couldn't answer, learning a short, simple answer and key verse if appropriate. Make sure you encourage the disciple and that all comments are constructive. Spend time praying about the experience and for the person the disciple shared with.

Debriefing allows us to improve a skill at a much greater rate because it brings things to our attention that we may never have noticed. Debriefing also rescues 'failures' and turns them into valuable learning experiences.

Reflection:

1. Can you think of any experiences in your life where you feel debriefing might have been helpful? Write some questions for that situation.
2. It is worthwhile experiencing debriefing from both sides. See if you can find someone to debrief you on the above situation or something else. If they are inexperienced you might first have to work out some questions together and then discuss them. Reverse the role and do the same for one of their experiences. Particularly useful experiences are something that you, or they, perceived as a 'failure'.

PART FOUR:

WHEN IS ENOUGH ENOUGH?

PART FOUR

What Is Enough
Enough

18: Should I Disciple Someone Forever?

If the aim of discipleship, as we said at the start, is Christian maturity, then the process never ends until we are in heaven. While it is true that we need to keep being discipled by Jesus throughout our lives, formal discipleship sessions with another believer may not go on that long. So how do we know when we should stop formally discipling another believer?

There are no set rules for how long one-to-one discipleship should last, but our aim as a discipler should be to move the disciple towards Christian maturity. If we have been meeting a new believer to teach them 'the basics', then this aim may be complete within six weeks, and they will be able to move on to other groups or discipleship programmes. If we are discipling a more mature believer, the individual may reach a stage where they do not need weekly Bible study with us and are competent and disciplined enough to study the Bible on their own. They may begin to prefer more informal discipleship such as simply spending time praying together. As you start to encourage your disciple in different acts of service, your discipleship may take the form of running outreach events together, leading other church groups or just acting as a sounding board when they need tips or advice. When discipling should cease is dependent on the situation. We need to be sensitive to the needs of the disciple and evolve our discipleship methods as the disciple grows.

Also we need to consider that as a disciple grows our help may no longer be suitable, but another Christian with different skills or experience may be required. Be prepared to hand a disciple on or suggest other ways they could get the help they need.

Reflection:

1. What level are you hoping to see your disciple reach? Where are they starting from? What are the key areas where they need to be bearing fruit for the discipling to have served its purpose?
2. What do you think are indicators that discipling should cease?

OTHER SOURCES OF INPUT

The reality is that every one of us has limitations. It is good for us to recognise these and to also recognise that a disciple will benefit from a wide range of input so they don't just become clones of us. If our disciple is growing and starting to need help in other areas, we should be prepared to pass them on to a new discipler who has the correct skills, or suggest other ways the disciple could continue learning. Such possibilities include:

Books

Expose the disciple to a wide range of thinking on a variety of topics. This will make sure we are not just pressing our own opinions or interpretations, will encourage the disciple to try to understand Scripture for themselves and will enable the disciple to get help in areas we may not be overly confident in. If this is the case then why not read a book together and take notes, or discuss sections?

Remember, though, disciples learn in different ways, and lots of independent reading may not be suitable for all types of learner.

Special Training

Workshops and seminars can encourage the disciple to learn from a wide range of people. They are especially good for practical skills training, as well as topical issues.

Ministry with Other Christians

Encouraging the disciple to work alongside others will give them a different perspective and will help them develop skills that we may not be so gifted at. Informal discipleship with other Christians can be very important and we should not be possessive of 'our' disciple.

Mixing with Others

Make sure the disciple is mixing with a range of Christians and non-Christians from different backgrounds. Meeting Christians from other churches and denominations challenges our own thinking and practices, and interacting with the secular world will face us with all kinds of challenges in terms of the Bible's teaching and its practical outworkings.

ONGOING CONTACT

Although the formal discipleship may cease, this needn't mean we have no further contact with the disciple, and much more informal discipleship may begin.

I used to work in a different town in Taiwan and while I worked there I discipled four women. When I moved two hours south, formal discipleship had to cease for practical reasons, but I still kept in touch with all four. It may be the occasional visit or letter, or more frequent emails and phone calls. If I am in town we arrange to meet up, usually over a meal in a quieter restaurant because our main purpose is to talk and pray together. Often in our sharing they will raise issues that they are struggling with, or questions they have about their ministry. Sometimes they write or telephone solely to discuss a current struggle, needing someone they can trust to listen and then pray for them. Sometimes they need help and I will point them to the appropriate Bible passages, leaving them to work out the answer with God's help and then ring me for any more discussion. The conversations leave us both encouraged and spurred on in our faith. Though a disciple may not need formal discipleship, most people find it very hard to continue the

Christian life without encouragements, however small. If we cease contact completely there is the risk they can drift slowly away from a close relationship with God or stop ministering to others. These women have led at least eight people to Christ and been involved in discipling other believers. Our ongoing contact spurs them on so that they don't get too busy and stop being involved in such vital ministries.

The Apostle Paul made three main missionary journeys, planting churches and discipling the new believers there. But it seems he only stayed in a place for a short period of time before moving on to a new region. The three places he stayed longest appear to be Rome (he was imprisoned there for a couple of years), Corinth (18 months) and Ephesus (two years). So how on earth did the new Christians get discipled?

Even at a distance it is evident that Paul kept praying for his disciples scattered throughout the Roman Empire and continued to disciple the new believers via letters. The letters were a key means of rebuking, correcting, reminding and encouraging the new Christians. Despite the limitations of communication 2,000 years ago, Paul was never cut off from those he discipled. Through prayer, follow-up visits, letters and personal ambassadors, he kept the links close. There was a network of ongoing care and encouragement. And it is much easier now than in Paul's era in terms of communication!

Reflection:

1. How could you maintain contact with those you have ministered with in the past? Think about what suits your situation and personality.

2. If you don't keep contact with previous disciples, what prevents you? What can be done about this?

19: PERSONAL DEBRIEF

We need to be continually evaluating how our discipleship is going and be prepared to make changes. Some people use the same methods year after year. They not only use the same methods, but they make the same mistakes. Keeping things the same may appear less work and less stress, but it is not going to help us grow, improve in our discipleship skills or pass on enthusiasm to those we are discipling.

Initially evaluation might need to be more formal. For some time I kept a notebook and evaluated all my discipleship experiences by spending 15 minutes writing about them. Later the evaluation became much more automatic. You might find it helpful to do evaluation with someone else who can help you see the situation from a different perspective.

A friend of mine, Justine, began her first attempt at discipling. After one week, she concluded she was a failure and should quit. Justine told me about her bad experience and we began to chat it through. I asked her some simple questions:

1. What went well? Why?
2. What went badly? Why?

3. Were there things that resulted in a poor experience? What were they? (e.g. environment, timing, choice of material, etc.).
4. How could you improve?

As we talked together a number of things became apparent:

Choice of disciple
Justine had approached a lady because someone else had asked her to. Though the lady claimed to be a Christian, it sounded like she had never made a commitment to Jesus, and was living with her boyfriend who was not at all interested in the gospel. The lady could have benefited from being discipled but was rather a challenge for a person only just starting to learn how to disciple others.

Boundaries
Justine hadn't set very good boundaries. She had agreed to an evening meeting for the other lady's convenience, but Justine had a young baby and the lady had talked and talked (mostly complaining) until midnight.

Content
Justine had tried to attempt far too much in her first sessions. She had tried to fit in two different Bible studies in one session. She noted, 'The lady listened well for the first section but seemed unable to pay attention in the second.' No wonder, if it was nearing midnight and they were covering so much information.

Talking through the experience, Justine realized she had set herself up for a bad experience and with some adjustments there was hope for future sessions.

It might turn out that Justine will not be able to keep meeting this lady because the lady might decide that she can't agree to the conditions of the relationship. It is not necessarily a failure to have to stop discipling someone. Often it is more of a failure to keep going in a bad situation.

There are instances when we may need to stop a discipleship relationship. Be aware of some of the following issues:

Problems of Disciple

Unwilling to learn

There are times to admit that a person is not yet suitable for discipling because they do not want to learn. They may be unwilling to answer questions, poor in attendance or lacking in concentration.

Unsuitable Discipler

We may not be a suitable person to disciple the individual. This could be because we are not confident enough in the areas they need help with, because our schedules are different or simply because we have a personality clash. In this case it is our responsibility to try to find them a suitable person.

Problems of Faith

Spiritual Dryness

Discipleship, like any ministry, is the result of the overflow from our own relationship with Jesus. If we are spiritually dry, then we cannot hope to encourage others or mature ourselves. If this is the case we need to review our own spiritual life. Are we the Sea of Galilee or the Dead Sea? If we have no input but are continually giving out, then we are very quickly going to become exhausted and frustrated.

Spiritual Attack

Satan hates discipling. He hates it because it produces mature and effective Christians, able to resist his power and influence. He will do everything and anything to try to prevent us from continuing. He is clever enough to know our weaknesses and will attack hard. We should expect that and be prepared to fight. But if we are struggling and tempted to sin, we need to be aware of this and consider whether we should be continuing in a teaching role.

PROBLEMS OF RELATIONSHIP

Dependence

A discipling relationship can be quite intense. It is relatively easy for a disciple to start saying 'My discipler says ...' It is important that our disciple is not becoming dependent on our explanations and interpretations, but is thinking for themselves and depending on the Holy Spirit. We need to constantly encourage the disciple to think of what God's Word says and to turn immediately to prayer. It may be as easy as just reminding them, 'Before you call me, first spend time praying and thinking about what God says on this issue,' or asking them what they think before expressing your own opinion. As the disciple matures we need to send them away more often so that they learn to depend on the Holy Spirit and not us. Our willingness to do this helps us check if our relationship is balanced or too dependent. Sometimes, though, you may have to take the more drastic step of making yourself unavailable to them as frequently as they want.

It can also be unhelpful for the discipler to be indirectly praised in this way. Pride is always lurking, and we may need to check our own motives for being involved in discipleship.

Inappropriate Attraction

The close relationship of discipleship can cause issues of inappropriate attraction, even homosexual attraction, to arise. This needs immediate action. It will usually mean ceasing to do one-to-one discipleship with the person, repentance and being accountable to someone who can help you work through the feelings. This issue doesn't mean that the person can never be involved in discipleship but group discipleship may be more suitable.

Authoritarianism or Control

Do we just want to feel useful and needed or to have control over another's behaviour? Discipling because you want people to be dependent on you or to have control over another person's life is not a healthy relationship, and the discipler needs to repent and think about their motives. Underlying issues such as low self-esteem or pride will need to be dealt with. Stopping discipleship may be necessary.

Personal Attachment

It is easy to become tied in to the successes and failures of the person we are discipling. If they grow well how easy it is to begin to think, 'I'm doing a wonderful job of discipling!' If their progress is slow we can easily get discouraged, thinking 'I must be hopeless at this!' Human beings are so 'me' focused. Though we need to make sure we are doing the best job we can, and are not doing anything to hinder the disciple's growth, we must remind ourselves over and over that neither success nor failure is ultimately related to us. It is God who brings growth. We are to be faithful in serving God but the results are His responsibility.

Problems of Method

Blindness to Issues

We are limited and weak human beings, and however much we pray, we cannot see into a disciple's heart and are likely to miss issues in their lives, especially if the disciple is doing well in other areas. Another perspective can quite often bring up issues that we have missed.

Learning Styles

If our disciple is a visual learner and we are a kinaesthetic learner, then we will want to approach study in different ways. This is not a barrier to discipleship but can take more effort, planning and thinking up suitable activities every week, and may lead to boredom on the disciple's part or miscommunication. We can easily find someone whom the disciple can relate to better.

We needn't be fearful, though, about being involved in discipleship. If we are aware of the dangers we will be alert and prepared to deal with them before they become a problem. We shouldn't think that stopping discipleship is failure either. It is better to stop a relationship than continue in a harmful or unfruitful way.

Reflection:

1. Evaluate one discipleship experience you've had. What were your overall impressions and conclusions? Were they reasonable conclusions or based on faulty thinking?
2. What questions could you ask yourself? Answer them.
3. What could you have done to improve your discipling?
4. Can you think of any other dangers and/or safeguards? What dangers do you think might be a problem for you? Why? What do you need to do about them?

Closing Note

Being involved in one-to-one discipleship is a privilege and joy. If I could only do one thing well then discipleship would be it. Done with a desire for God's glory it will stimulate your Christian life and leave you astonished at what God can do.

Recently I met a family that God has been gradually bringing to Himself over the past six years. Justine was in her mid-20s when a teacher at her college led her to the Lord. For a while that teacher continued to disciple Justine. I was discipling the teacher, so she would often ask for my guidance on various issues. One issue was that Justine had become ensnared in a pyramid selling scheme and felt very uncomfortable with the ethics of it. Eventually, through prayer and the teacher's assistance, she managed to get out of the scheme. Justine learnt a lot through that whole experience. Shortly afterwards the teacher had to stop discipling Justine so I took over. That first year we did an Old Testament overview, Ephesians and basic evangelism training. During that year we became firm friends and would often meet for meals and discuss the Bible and its practical application. We'd also telephone each other and pray for each other. I was introduced to Justine's non-Christian boyfriend, Stephen, and we were able to have a useful gospel conversation together.

More than a year later we asked Stephen if he'd like to learn more about the Bible together. We met every week for several months and did a Bible overview and then Luke and Acts. Justine was able to observe evangelism being done and to increasingly participate as I deferred to her for answers. Stephen asked many intelligent questions.

However I then moved to a town over two hours away where I was involved in planting a new church and I couldn't meet up regularly with Justine. Even though we couldn't see each other as often, we would still chat on the phone and spend the odd weekend visiting each other. Whatever we were doing we would always take time to talk about the gospel and practical Christianity, discussing issues we were facing and encouraging each other to keep on track with God.

Justine chose to marry her boyfriend even though he was not yet a Christian. The church that led the wedding did such a good job of the service that her husband's brother and his wife decided to investigate Christianity for themselves. They bravely took the first step in attending church and soon were convinced about God's love for them. Meanwhile Justine's younger sister, seeing the changes in Justine's life, had also decided to investigate Christianity and soon became a Christian too. And just about a year after they were married, Justine's husband Stephen finally submitted to Jesus.

Justine's brother Andrew and sister Judy also started attending church. But being pressurized to attend lots of meetings they were quickly put off. Someone tried to meet each of them on a one-to-one basis, but both felt the study rather irrelevant and too generalised to really deal with any of their issues. Frustrated, they gave up on the church.

It isn't that the Christians didn't want to help but rather that they didn't know how to deal with people who didn't fit into their existing programmes and structures.

I didn't know how I could help, living so far away, but offered to meet up and chat with each of them.

Andrew was 27 and a dancer. He thought deeply and tended to be much more emotional. Judy was 36 years old and divorced. She was really just interested in joining the church choir and hadn't grasped any of the gospel.

I met up with them several times over a few months, just taking a couple of hours each time I was visiting to chat with them and answer their questions. I gave them sections of the Bible to read in between my visits. They asked lots of good questions and found that God was answering their prayers. Eventually both became Christians and were baptized. Andrew has since led his girlfriend to the Lord. Both now attend church and are much more able to fit into the programmes and welcome other newcomers like them.

My relationship with Justine and her family still continues but the methods keep evolving as different situations and requirements arise.

I pray that God will equip you to be involved in discipling and that you will see God producing fruit through this ministry of multiplication just as I have.

Appendix a

Nebuchadnezzar Case Study (p. 64)

1. Nebuchadnezzar's 'bricks':
   - There are many gods.
   - Babylon's gods must be the most powerful because Babylon is the most powerful country. Thus, Israel's gods must be weak because they were defeated.
   - The gods communicate with this world but you need mediators (magicians etc.) to interpret, especially the dreams and omens.

2. Nebuchadnezzar is a long way from believing in the God of the Bible; he is on the far left of the link diagram.

3. Nebuchadnezzar seems to be a non-believer because:
   - 2:46: He falls on the ground to worship Daniel rather than his God.
   - 2:47: He refers to God as 'God of gods'. There is no concept of there only being one God. Rather, God is the most powerful of many.
   - He refers to God as 'your' god (no feeling that the king has a connection with this god).
   - 3:1: He immediately makes a huge idol and forces people to worship it and follow his will or they will die.

- There is no tolerance then for Daniel's friends and their worship of the God who has already done a huge miracle in his life.
- 3:28-29: Sounds like progress but still God is the God of others, not himself.

4. He is still on the left hand side of the diagram (still an unbeliever), although he is hopefully moving in a positive direction as he learns more about God.

5. Nebuchadnezzar believes that he is the centre of the universe. He attributes all that he has done to his own hard work and reveals that he has done it for his own glory. He is proud and refuses to acknowledge God as the King and centre of the universe.

6. Nebuchadnezzar seems to be a believer because:
- 4:34: The king was told he'd be a beast until he acknowledged God as King. God obviously accepts him as fulfilling this condition. 'Raising of his eyes' is a reference to submission to a greater King.
- He praises and glorifies God who lives forever. Sounds real and personal.
- 4:34-35: Sounds like a real prayer, and he acknowledges many things he never would before, including recognizing that all people (including himself) are nothing compared to God, and God has the right to do anything, including humiliating judgments.
- 4:37: Now the king himself implies a personal relationship with God (v. 2 – note the 'me'). He acknowledges that God has the right to humble the proud.
- 4:1: This whole chapter is actually a letter written to everyone in his kingdom. It shows a concern for others to also know God. It is a testimony and quite a humiliating one at that. Kings of his day would never admit their humiliations and 'lose face' as he did. To me this is one of the strongest evidences, as he does not cover up his sin but acknowledges it when everyone else would have said, 'what's wrong with pride, you are great'.

Appendix B

Case Studies (p. 67)
These are possible suggestions. Each question could be asked in many ways. There is great flexibility depending on the circumstances and your relationship with a person.

Case Study 1:
Julie, a lady in her 20s who replied 'I haven't been baptized yet' when asked if she was a Christian.

Possible 'Bricks'
- She's not good enough to be baptized.
- Being a Christian is mostly about the good work of baptism.
- Baptism is a higher level of being a Christian and she just wants to be an 'ordinary'-level Christian because that seems less difficult.
- One is not acceptable to God without baptism.

Provisional Diagnosis
- She may not be a Christian.
- She may be a brand-new Christian who hasn't had baptism explained well.

Possible Clarifying Questions
- How does someone become a Christian?
- How would you explain what baptism is?
- Why would someone get baptized?
- What happens to someone who chooses to follow Jesus but doesn't get baptized? See Luke 23:39-43 for a man who didn't have the opportunity to be baptized but was clearly headed for heaven.

Case Study 2:
Esther's family came to faith when she was a teenager. She is now 40 and married to a non-Christian. Esther has started meeting me regularly to do Bible study and has started coming to church every week.

Possible 'Bricks'
- Becoming a Christian is no different to choosing to be vegetarian; just follow the group decision (motive?).
- Churchgoing is 'good' and will impress God or the family.
- Agreeing to do Bible study to appease family or impress someone.
- Lots of possible misunderstandings about what a Christian is.
- Also perhaps confusion about the difference being a Christian makes to our choices and why marrying a non-Christian was not a good choice.

Provisional Diagnosis
- A non-Christian who just went along with the family decision without really understanding or choosing it for herself.
- Possibly a Christian who was never discipled and so made the foolish decision (perhaps in ignorance) of marrying a non-Christian.

Possible Clarifying Questions
- How did the family become Christian and what did you believe at the time?
- What makes someone a Christian?
- Why have you decided to come to church now?
- What are you learning at church? Or what do you notice?

N.B. There is little point in talking about her previous decision as it can't be changed.

Case Study 3:
A man I met in a non-Christian setting who quickly told me he was a Roman Catholic who went to Mass each week.

Possible 'Bricks'
- Might think God or even just I would be impressed by his fervent attendance at Mass. Perhaps this is his way of stopping any further conversation!
- Getting right with God involves good works like Mass attendance.
- He is an above-average 'good' guy.
- There is no need for further conversation as his commitment is made.

Provisional Diagnosis
- Most likely doesn't know Jesus or understand salvation by grace but trusts in his good works.
- Possibly a believer who is confused by grace and works.

Possible Clarifying Questions
- Why do you go to Mass?
- What do you think will get you into heaven?
- Clarify what he is trusting in.
- Why did Jesus have to come to die?

This conversation took place at a petrol station in New Zealand. He clearly confirmed he was trusting in his good deeds to save him. The last question was met with silence and then, 'It doesn't make sense for Jesus to die for me if I could save myself, does it?' We then were able to have an excellent conversation about grace and how to know Jesus.

Case Study 4:
Caroline, a new Christian, attends a house church with her husband and children. But she has taken her sick child to a faith healer.

Possible 'Bricks'
- Perhaps has never occurred to her to ask Jesus for healing or thinks it is presumptuous or doesn't happen today.
- Jesus' role is to heal and make everything easy. If He doesn't, then we turn to other solutions.
- Jesus is just one source of help and there is nothing wrong with trying the faith healer.
- She's just desperate and not thinking clearly.
- It's just a habit to turn to the faith healer and she never thought of Jesus as interested in her child's health.

Provisional Diagnosis
- Perhaps isn't a Christian but most likely is just a baby believer who hasn't been taught on these issues.

Possible Clarifying Questions
Remember that Caroline is likely to be tired, worried and desperate. Approaching the issue obliquely will help. Being concerned, asking what you can do to help and praying for the family might be what is appropriate at the moment of crisis. Gentle questions might reveal the bricks and guide you as to how to encourage her to follow God's way.

- 'Could you tell me what's happened?' She will quite likely reveal her thinking on why she went to the healer without being asked directly.
- What difference might it make being a Christian when your child is sick?
- At a later opportunity (once the child is out of danger), ask about what happens if we go to faith healers? (i.e. the implications of that choice on the child, their faith and witness…).

Case Study 5:
John, his wife and five children are active in a Catholic charismatic group. They seem to have come to faith in Jesus and have destroyed their idols. He feels sure he will go to heaven because he has not committed a major sin.

Possible 'Bricks'
- Having idols was a major sin and getting rid of them proves he's 'good'.
- Sounds like he's depending on good works for salvation.
- God can be impressed by things we do.

Provisional Diagnosis
- Might not yet be a Christian.
- A new believer who isn't yet well taught and is confused about grace and works (which is very difficult for people to grasp).

Possible Clarifying Questions
- Why did he destroy the idols (this will help you know what else to ask)?
- How can someone get to heaven?
- What impresses God?
- What does he mean by major sin? What does the Bible say about sin?
- Obviously there will need to be a simple explanation of grace given and applied to the situation.

Case Study 6:
A young married couple who live with his parents are new Christians and were attending church. But his mother threatened to kick them out if they kept going, so they no longer attend.

Possible 'Bricks'
- Perhaps they think being a Christian should be easy and that family opposition proves they've made the wrong decision.
- Maybe they believe they can be Christians and not meet up with others and still remain strong.
- Must submit to in-laws, and this means total obedience.
- There could be any number of reasons for what has happened, ranging from misconceptions to fear, or simply thinking slowly and praying about what to do. Don't jump in with hasty judgments.

Provisional Diagnosis
- Perhaps rethinking their decision.
- New believers not sure what to do or making the wrong decisions.
- Already quite mature believers who are on the way to a mature solution to the situation!

Possible Clarifying Questions
- Show love and concern and try to speak to them away from their home and ask how they're getting on as Christians.
- What challenges are they facing?
- How are they dealing with them?
- How can you help?

Appendix C

Reflection (p. 76)

For each of the disciples below, choose a suitable Bible book to study.

1.   A person who has made a 'decision' at a meeting but has little grasp of sin or salvation. You're not even sure whether they are a Christian.

Suggestions:
General Bible overview
Luke – talk about how Jesus dealt with sin

2.   A new Christian who has many bad habits from their past life.

Suggestions:
We may be tempted to do topical Bible studies with him on each of his 'problems', but a less direct approach will be much better and far less likely to develop a legalistic person. The key, as always, is not to try to force 'fruit' to grow, but to nurture the roots and let the Holy Spirit work. As the person grows to love Jesus more, their sin will become increasingly obvious to them. Perhaps try a Bible overview, a Gospel like Matthew, which is particularly challenging in its radical ethics or a book like Ephesians, which gets us excited about the gospel and

then gives application in how we should respond to such a wonderful gospel.

3.   A new Christian who has never learnt how to relate to people.

Suggestions:
Good relationships are the fruit of nourished roots. Anything that helps them to understand God and how He relates to us. Possibly Ephesians or Romans or parts of Corinthians.

4.   A new believer who is being swayed by the legalistic teachings of a cult.

Suggestions:
This believer needs to be reminded of the gospel, so choose anything that goes over the basics of salvation. Possibilities include Genesis 1-3, making sure they understand what sin is, or John's Gospel, looking at who Jesus claimed to be and how we can become 'children of God'. It has lots of good material in it about 'good' people who thought they were saved. Galatians was written to demonstrate that there is no 'gospel plus works'; or Ephesians 2 may be good.

5.   A Muslim-background believer who is familiar with the Quran but not the Bible.

Suggestions:
It is a good idea to take the individual from what they already know. As the Quran refers to Jesus and Old Testament figures, it may be easier to go from that to what the Bible says. It is important to get to know the individual first so as to avoid things that will unnecessarily offend them. You don't want to set up any barriers before you start which will distract from the message you are sharing.

For example, you will need to use a Bible that is obviously looked after and clear of handwritten notes and underlining. If your Bible is marked or placed on the floor, they will view you as someone who doesn't treat God's Word with reverence and they will struggle to respect anything you're saying. Ask someone who knows a little about cultural issues or read an appropriate book that will help you avoid some pitfalls. You could try an Old Testament overview, perhaps in depth on Genesis to Exodus, emphasizing sin and the fact that we are 'dead' and cannot do anything to save ourselves. Once a firm foundation has been laid, something like Matthew, which relates a lot to the Old Testament and shows how Jesus fulfils it, would be a good progression.

Many Muslim-background believers may already have a good knowledge of the Bible before they become a Christian, because they have spent a long time investigating the Bible and considering whether they are willing to pay the high cost of conversion.

6.   A new church leader in a church that lacks leadership and a helpful structure.

Suggestions:
Acts, Timothy and/or Titus

7.   A mature believer who has suffered tremendous personal loss.

Suggestions:
This person needs to know that they are not alone and that God loves them. Our care of them and willingness to spend time with them will be particularly important. Possibilities include the Gospels, looking particularly at the loss Jesus went through and why He was willing to go through this; Paul's life (Acts), or Philippians which is so joyful, despite Paul being in jail; or 1 Peter, which is written to a church under great pressure

8.   A once missions-minded church has become very internally focused and you're discipling one of the church leaders.

Suggestions:
Looking at God's purposes throughout the Bible, and getting them excited about the gospel themselves. Acts, as an expression of the Great Commission, could be a good topic for study.

9.   A new believer who is not very clear on their own beliefs and is in danger of being deceived.

Suggestions:
Genesis 1-3 is helpful in laying the foundations, as are the Gospels or Romans 1-8. Galatians, where even Peter was getting off track, may be helpful.

10. A family led to faith recently but non-committal about attending church.

Suggestions:
My personal experience is that if we get people excited about Jesus, they will naturally begin to get involved in a local church. Talking about why we go to church could help, and Acts gives a picture of how the church was designed to function.

11. Someone being persecuted and wanting to give up.

Suggestions:
Acts, Philippians and 1 Peter all deal with perseverance despite difficulty.

12. A Jewish-background believer with skewed or limited under-standing of the Old Testament.

Suggestions:
Perhaps an overview of Old Testament, focusing on how it points forward to Jesus and God's eternal purpose. Matthew's Gospel was written specifically for those from a Jewish background.

13. A Roman Catholic-background believer.

Suggestions:
An overview of the Bible with a clear focus on sin and necessity for Jesus. You might need to do a special session on Mary. Hebrews, which emphasises that Jesus died once for all time and is now our only mediator, may be helpful in addressing the biblical view of priests. Anything emphasizing grace would also be helpful, such as Ephesians or Romans 1-8.

Appendix D

Learning Methods for Different Types of Disciple (p. 87)

Visual:
Reading, Research, e-learning, Observing, Drawing, Mind Maps, Videos, Drama, Writing poetry, Goal-setting and Case studies.

Auditory:
Group discussion, Lectures, Feedback, Coaching, Videos, Question and Answer sessions, Writing music, Goal-setting and Case studies.

Kinaesthetic:
On-the-job evangelism, Coaching in an active way, Role playing, Writing music or poetry, Drama, Goal-setting and Case studies.

Appendix E

Chapter 13: Dealing with Tough Issues

Case Studies (p. 99)

1.

Mark is a successful businessman who became a Christian two years ago and has grown steadily. But he still mistreats his employees. He pays them poorly and often scolds them. Unsurprisingly, he has not led any of them to faith.

Your approach will be affected by your relationship with the disciple.

- Studying Ephesians or 1 Peter together will let the issue come up in the course of the study.
- Don't accuse but ask questions to help them think about their behaviour themselves. You could ask questions like, 'How should a Christian employer be different to a non-Christian?' or 'How do you think an employer could influence his employees so that they also become Christians?'
- Use a testimony if this area was a struggle for you or someone you know, or think through a 'parable' together of an employee turned off the gospel because of their employer's behaviour.

2.

Rachel is one of the top teachers in the local high school. She came to faith six months ago and has noticed that most members of the church do not study the Bible as seriously as she does. She complains to you about their lack of commitment.

Same principles as above.
- Share a personal testimony about your struggles and how you have dealt with them.
- Ask why she thinks people might have different levels of apparent commitment. Look at issues such as lack of time, too many other responsibilities, lack of confidence, poor reading skills and so on.
- Look at Matthew 7:1-5, and ask questions about what Jesus means and why He says this.

3.

Deborah has been a faithful church member for several years. However, she does not have a spiritual gift that brings her much attention. You have just discovered that she sometimes spreads gossip about leaders whom she envies.

Low self-esteem is the likely cause of this problem, and dealing with this 'root' problem is best.
- Study Ephesians, perhaps focusing on who we are in Christ.
- Share a testimony of how God changed you in this area.
- Explain the 'sword of the Spirit' and choose appropriate passages or concepts to memorise.
- Consider the purpose of spiritual gifts, the focus on others and the aim to build up the body. Look at how God has gifted each differently and what jealousy of others implies that we are saying to God.

4.

Sarah is the mother of five children. Her husband is a casual labourer whose employment is spasmodic. Sarah cannot always meet the basic needs of their children, so she frequently buys a lottery ticket in the hope of winning a large sum of money that will help them out.

The issue here is related to lack of trust in God to supply our needs and trying to find our own methods.

- Look at passages such as Matthew 6:19-34 and ask what it means and how it applies.
- Ask if she believes God truly loves her and is trustworthy. Discuss why she is buying a lottery ticket, and what does it imply she believes about God?
- Look at the practicalities – the probability of winning the lottery and how much could be saved by not buying a ticket.
- Share a testimony of when you were tempted not to trust God and how this issue was dealt with.

5.

Jack is a high-school student. He is often tempted to visit websites with sexually explicit material. He has just admitted to you that he now daydreams often about having sex with his girlfriend.

- Share a testimony of someone who got involved with pornography and how the issue was resolved. Remember to assure them that God can forgive and help them change.
- Discuss why God wants us to be pure. Think through the dangers of pornography.
- Discuss ways together to help each other with this issue. How can you be accountable to each other? You might come up with different methods for each of you.
- Consider using books or other resources if you really don't feel able to handle the issue. Or see if they would prefer to talk over the issue with someone else who perhaps has more experience in dealing with the issue.

OMF International works in most East Asian countries, and among East Asian peoples around the world. It was founded by James Hudson Taylor in 1865 as the China Inland Mission. Our purpose is to glorify God through the urgent evangelisation of East Asia's billions.

In line with this, OMF Publishing seeks to motivate and equip Christians to make disciples of all peoples. Publications include:

- stories and biographies showing God at work in East Asia
- the biblical basis of mission and mission issues
- the growth and development of the Church in Asia
- studies of Asian culture and religion

Books, booklets, articles and free downloads can be found on our web site at www.omf.org

English-Speaking OMF Centres

Australia: PO Box 849, Epping, NSW 1710
Tel: 02 9868 4777 email: au@omf.net www.au.omf.org

Canada: 5155 Spectrum Way, Building 21, Mississauga, ONT L4W 5A1
Toll free: 1 888 657 8010 email: omfcanada@omf.ca www.ca.omf.org

Hong Kong: PO Box 70505, Kowloon Central PO, Hong Kong
Tel: 852 2398 1823 email: hk@omf.net www.omf.org.hk

Malaysia: 3A Jalan Nipah, off Jalan Ampang, 55000, Kuala Lumpur
Tel: 603 4257 4263 email: my@omf.net www.omf.org.my

New Zealand: PO Box 10159, Dominion Road, Balmoral, Auckland, 1030
Tel: 09 630 5778 email: omfnz@omf.net www.nz.omf.org

Philippines: QCCPO Box 1997-1159, 1100 Quezon City, M.M.
Tel: 632 951 0782 email: ph-hc@omf.net www.omf.org

Singapore: 2 Cluny Road, Singapore 259570
Tel: 65 6475 4592 email: sno@omf.net www.sg.omf.org

UK: Station Approach, Borough Green, Sevenoaks, Kent TN15 8BG
Tel: 01732 887299 email: omf@omf.org.uk www.omf.org.uk

USA: 10 West Dry Creek Circle, Littleton, CO 80120-4413
Toll free: 1 800 422 5330 email: omfus@omf.org www.omf.org/us

OMF International Headquarters:2 Cluny Road, Singapore 259570
Tel: 65 6319 4550 email: ihq@omf.net www.omf.org

Christian Focus Publications
publishes books for all ages

Books in our adult range are published in three imprints.
Christian Focus contains popular works including biographies, commentaries, basic doctrine and Christian living. Our children's books are also published in this imprint.
Mentor focuses on books written at a level suitable for Bible College and seminary students, pastors, and other serious readers. The imprint includes commentaries, doctrinal studies, examination of current issues and church history.
Christian Heritage contains classic writings from the past.

Christian Focus Publications, Ltd
Geanies House, Fearn,
Ross-shire, IV20 1TW, Scotland.
info@christianfocus.com

Our titles are available from
www.christianfocus.com